New York Beauties

QUILTS FROM THE EMPIRE STATE

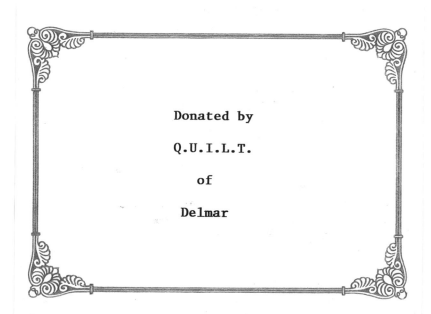

1. Detail of Mariner's Compass; made by Emeline Barker (1820–1906); New York City; date unknown; pieced and appliquéd cotton. The complete quilt is illustrated on page 121. (Collection of the Museum of the City of New York 44.318; Bequest of Mrs. Marian Place Hildrith)

New York Beauties

QUILTS FROM THE EMPIRE STATE

Jacqueline M. Atkins

and

Phyllis A. Tepper

Research Coordinator
Lee Kogan

Dutton Studio Books New York
In association with the
Museum of American Folk Art New York

DUTTON STUDIO BOOKS

Published by the Penguin Group
Penguin Books USA Inc., 375 Hudson Street,
New York, New York 10014, U.S.A.

Penguin Books Ltd, 27 Wrights Lane,
London W8 5TZ, England

Penguin Books Australia Ltd, Ringwood,
Victoria, Australia

Penguin Books Canada Ltd, 2801 John Street,
Markham, Ontario, Canada L3R 1B4

Penguin Books (N.Z.) Ltd, 182-190 Wairau Road,
Auckland 10, New Zealand

Penguin Books Ltd, Registered Offices:
Harmondsworth, Middlesex, England

First Published by Dutton Studio Books, an imprint of Penguin Books USA Inc.

First printing, June, 1992
10 9 8 7 6 5 4 3 2 1

Library of Congress
Catalog Card Number 92-71074

Printed and bound by Dai Nippon Printing Co, Ltd., Tokyo, Japan
Book designed by Marilyn Rey

Unless otherwise noted, the photographs of the quilts in this book were taken by Scott Bowron.

ISBN: 0-525-93432-4 (cloth); ISBN: 0-525-48598-8 (DP)

Dedicated to the memory of Robert Bishop,
our friend and mentor

Contents

Acknowledgments

A project such as the New York Quilt Project had to depend on many people to accomplish its objectives. To each and every one involved, we give our heartfelt thanks for the time and energy given so graciously and unstintingly.

To Folk Art Institute students for research and administration aid: Mercedes Bierman, Joan Bloom, Sheila Brummel, Nancy Fischer, Diane Hill, Caroline Hohenrath, Lynne Ingram, Barbara Klinger, Carolyn Kuhlthau, Paula Laverty, Martha Leversuch, Fran Lieu, Carmen Mercadel, Suzanne Murphy, Jeanne Riger, Phyllis Selnick, Mimi Sherman, Sarah Snook, Lynne Steuer, Yolanda Van de Krol.

To Museum of American Folk Art staff who advised and aided in administrative tasks: Didi Barrett, Beth Bergin, Catherine Dunworth, Susan Flamm, Alice Hoffman, Stacy Hollander, Eileen Jear, Johleen Nester, Cathy Rasmussen, Ann-Marie Reilly, Ralph Sessions, Lucille Stiger, Elizabeth V. Warren.

To curators, town historians, librarians, archivists, quilt historians, quilt dealers, and textile conservators, who answered questions and facilitated research: Barbara Austin, Suffolk County Historical Society; Cuesta Benberry; Doris Bowman, Smithsonian Institution; Barbara Brackman; Ruthanne Brod, New York State Museum; Joanne Brooks, Suffolk County Historical Society; Betty Chichester, Town Historian of Broome, Schoharie County; Varick Chittenden, Traditional Arts in Upstate New York, Inc.; Nancy Clokey; Reverend Warren Danskin, 44 John Street United Methodist Church; Henry Duffy, Lyndhurst; John Eilertsen, Hallockville Folk Art Museum; Clyde Eller, Buffalo-Erie County Historical Society; Shirley Eng, Fashion Institute of Technology; Judith L. Estes, Society for Preservation of Long Island Antiquities; Lynn Felsher, Fashion Institute of Technology; Laura Fisher; Kenneth Hasbrouck, Huguenot Historical Society of New Paltz; Mary Iannone, Amherst Museum; Marilynn Karp, Anonymous Arts Recovery Society; Dorothy King, East Hampton Free Library; Jane Bentley Kolter; Kate and Joel Kopp, America Hurrah Antiques; Desiree Koslin, Fashion Institute of Technology; Elizabeth Leckie, Van Cortlandt House; Lowell McAllister, Frederic Remington Art Museum; Amy McKune, The Museums at Stony Brook; Gillian Moss, Cooper Hewitt Museum; Shannon O'Dell, Dewitt Historical Society of Tompkins County; Celia Y. Oliver, Shelburne Museum; Susan Parrish; Vickie Paullus, The Stearns Technical Textiles Company; Mary Ellen Perry, Margaret Woodbury Strong Museum; Wesley Prieb, Tabor College, Hillsboro, Kansas; Lisa Roman, New York Academy of Sciences (successor organization to the American Institute); Eugene P. Sheehy, Museum of American Folk Art; Carol Traynor, Society for the Preservation of Long Island Antiquities; Nancy Tuckhorn, Daughters of the American Revolution Museum; Alson Van Wagner, Haviland Archives; Deborah Waters, Museum of the City of New York; Gail Doering Weimer, Oneida Community Mansion House; Marion Weston, Fashion Institute of Technology; and to the staff librarians at the New-York Historical Society and the New York Public Library.

To Museum of American Folk Art volunteers and interns who performed administrative chores so necessary to help the Project keep its time commitments: Donna Boyle, Sarah Cantine, Bernice Cohen, Tom Cuff, Jane diBernardo, Judy Doenias, Kim Hull, Judith Lawlor, Gillian Morris, Beverly Riesberg, Diana Robinson, Angie Roth, Marjorie Schnader, Diane Schneck, Judy Shapiro, Myra Shaskan, Irving Tepper, Linda Vredenburgh, and Xiaoyan Zhang.

Gratitude and thanks are extended to the following people for their very special and unique contributions to the New York Quilt Project:

Dr. Robert Bishop, the late Director of the Museum of American Folk Art, for his knowledge, vision, and advice.

Gerard C. Wertkin, Director of the Museum of American Folk Art, for his support at all stages of the New York Quilt Project.

Barbara Cate, Director of the Folk Art Institute, for her counsel, encouragement, and readiness to make the Institute available to the needs of the Project.

Lee Kogan, Assistant Director of the Folk Art Institute, for her continuous presence in various capacities.

Edith Wise, Librarian of the Museum of American Folk Art, for always finding the right source.

Irma J. Shore, for her participation as co-director until 1988, when she left to head Access to Art.

Tracy Cate, for his generous contribution to the photography for the New York Quilt Project.

Laura Lopata, for cataloguing the Project's archival material.

Sarah Snook, for developing the data base for archival storage of quilt documentation.

Jeffrey Gutcheon, for those endless yards of fabric donated to the volunteer documentors at Quilt Days.

Shelly Zegart, for the inspiration to begin the Project.

Laurel Horton, for advice on conducting oral interviews.

Deborah Blincoe, for training of volunteer documentors.

Cyril I. Nelson, for his special quilt connoisseurship.

Scott Bowron, for photography emphasizing each quilt's beauty and to Gavin Ashworth, for additional photography of objects included in the book.

Ann Kiewel, of the Lower Hudson Conference, for disseminating information about the New York Quilt Project.

This Project would have been impossible without the regional coordinators. Special thanks to Aurelie Stack for organizing the Long Island region; Anna-Marie Tucker for organizing the Catskill and upper Hudson Valley regions; Edith Mitchell for organizing the North Country region; Diane Sutherland for organizing the mid-Central and Southern Tier regions; and Nancilu Burdick for organizing the western New York State counties. Appendix I is an acknowledgment to the guilds and the area coordinators, as well as organizations donating space in which to hold quilt days.

The quilt owners who brought in their quilts deserve special accolades for preserving them and being willing to share their beauty and stories with us.

To our husbands, Edward G. Atkins and Irving Tepper, whose love and constant support made this book possible.

Foreword

The New York Quilt Project is dedicated to a remarkable group of artists who created a significant body of folk art through the use of traditional tools: needle, thread, and fabric. Through tireless handiwork and creative energy they have warmed generations of beds and hearts, and in the process have left a magnificent legacy. As one of the country's first colonies to be settled on the eastern seaboard, New York State has a long and distinguished cultural history. Among the well known artistic contributions from the state, the American public has come to appreciate the work of the limners who painted the patroon families of the Hudson Valley, the naturalists who found inspiration in the state's physical splendor, and contemporary artists who today give Manhattan much of its vitality. Into this distinguished company we now welcome the quiltmakers of New York State in recognition of their artistic skills.

The Museum of American Folk Art has played a leading role for many years in bringing American quilts to the public's attention by collecting and exhibiting them in the United States and abroad. Thus, it became a mission of the Museum, as a New York institution, to initiate the New York Quilt Project and locate, document, preserve, and create an archive for the quilts of its home state. The Museum's Folk Art Institute was the logical vehicle for carrying out this mission. Phyllis A. Tepper, Registrar and a graduate of the Institute, and a Fellow of the Museum of American Folk Art, as well as a quiltmaker herself with an active interest in American needlework, became the director of the Project. As such she was responsible for its planning, organization, and administration. She was asked to publish the findings, curate an exhibition, and create the archive for the Museum. This book is the ongoing progress report of the work of the New York Quilt Project, and it is the collaborative effort of Phyllis A. Tepper, her co-author, Jacqueline M. Atkins, and Lee Kogan, Research Coordinator for the Project.

Parameters for the documentation of quilts made in New York State were set from the earliest quilt located—it was signed and dated in 1753—to 1940. This latter date was chosen because it was a convenient historical turning point and sufficient data could still be amassed to permit the objectives of the New York Quilt Project to be accomplished.

The Museum of American Folk Art has a mandate to provide the public with the latest and best knowledge based on solid research and scholarship. There were certain risks entailed in a project of this nature. Would the public bring in quilts for documentation? Would all areas of the state be represented? Would a representative cross-section of the people of the state be obtained? We believe that the premises and objectives set forth have been met, and certain important gaps have now been identified for further research.

Because of the nature of the research motivated by the New York Quilt Project, certain attributions are now being corrected and/or confirmed. For example, it appears that the Pieties Quilt made by Maria Cadman Hubbard in 1848 can now be attributed to New York State rather than to New England as had formerly been believed. Research is in progress to pinpoint the county in which it was made.

The archives have already produced data for an article about unquilted tops in seven of the western counties of the state that has been written by Barbara Phillippi, one of the local western New York coordinators, published by the American Quilt Study Group. We believe that a great deal of work remains to be done, but we feel that the Museum has provided the motivation and tools for continuing this research. The Museum's publications, *The Clarion*, America's Folk Art Magazine, and *The Quilt Connection*, its newsletter devoted solely to quilts, will continue to publish articles and findings motivated by the New York Quilt Project archives.

Dr. Robert Bishop
Director, 1977–1991
Museum of American Folk Art

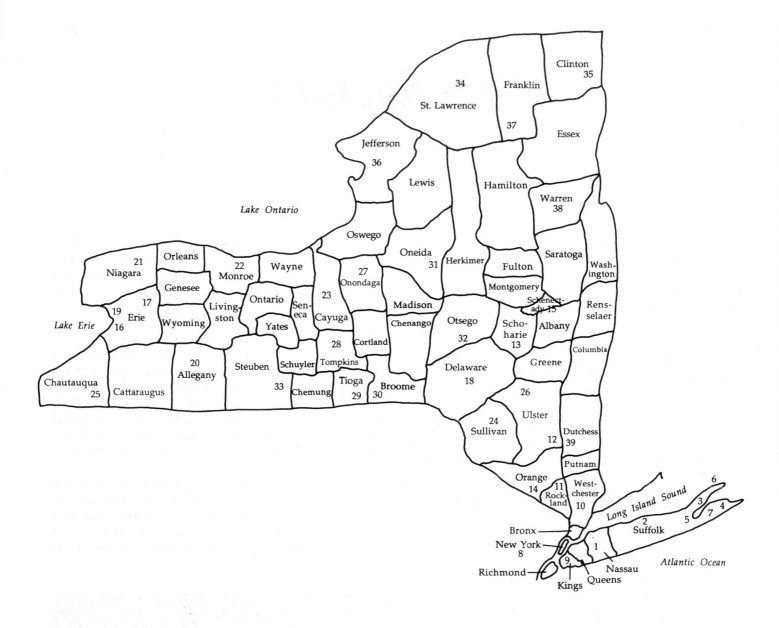

1. Hempstead, Nassau County
2. Stony Brook, Suffolk County
3. Peconic, Suffolk County
4. East Hampton, Suffolk County
5. Riverhead, Suffolk County
6. Orient, Suffolk County
7. Southampton, Suffolk County
8. Manhattan, New York County
9. Brooklyn, Kings County
10. Somers, Westchester County
11. Thiells, Rockland County
12. Marlboro, Ulster County
13. Warnerville, Schoharie County

14. Warwick, Orange County
15. Schenectady, Schenectady County
16. Hamburg, Erie County
17. Amherst, Erie County
18. Hamden, Delaware County
19. Buffalo, Erie County
20. Belfast, Allegany County
21. Lockport, Niagara County
22. Rochester, Monroe County
23. Auburn, Cayuga County
24. Liberty, Sullivan County
25. Jamestown, Chautauqua County
26. Stone Ridge, Ulster County

27. Syracuse, Onondaga County
28. Ithaca, Tompkins County
29. Owego, Tioga County
30. Vestal, Broome County
31. Utica, Oneida County
32. Oneonta, Otsego County
33. Corning-Painted Post, Steuben County
34. Potsdam, St. Lawrence County
35. Plattsburgh, Clinton County
36. Watertown, Jefferson County
37. Tupper Lake, Franklin County
38. Glens Falls, Warren County
39. Wappingers Falls, Dutchess County

2. Map of New York State that shows the counties and the cities and towns cited in this book.

Introduction

My background did not include quilts other than those feather quilts from my childhood that had been part of my mother's heritage. However, when working as a docent at the Museum of American Folk Art, I began to learn about the American quilt tradition and I loved the wonderful art of so many of them. This was about the time of the Bicentennial. During this time, I witnessed a quilting demonstration at Hallmark's store at Fifth Avenue and 56th Street, and I fell in love with the lively pattern stretched on a quilting frame that was being quilted by four women. I stayed so long that the curiosity of one of the quiltmakers was aroused enough for her to ask why. I told her that I was fascinated by the visual appeal of the quilt on the frame and would love to be able to do that kind of needlework. She was kind enough to tell me about Josie McKinley, a quilt teacher in my neighborhood. I promptly enrolled in a quilt course taught through an adult-education program at a local high school, and I have been happily working with quilts ever since.

I have always been interested in the history and culture of my native state, and it seemed natural to me to want to explain how and why women made quilts, how they developed their patterns, and how they formed their aesthetic judgments as to what made a beautiful quilt. Shelly Zegart, in a lecture at a symposium of Southern Folk Art sponsored by the Museum of American Folk Art in the summer of 1985, set my thought processes in motion. Her description of the Kentucky Quilt Project showed me that by examining the quilts of my native state, I might be able to find some answers to some of my questions. Because of my association with the Folk Art Institute, the Museum of American Folk Art became the sponsor of such a search and the New York Quilt Project was born.

A course of planning and organization then took place. A distinguished panel of consultants was assembled to help in the development of the Project's objectives and to give guidance to Museum staff and Institute students and volunteers who worked on the Project. Chosen were Robert Bishop, Director of the Museum of American Folk Art, an authority on quilts and author of many books

about quilts; Deborah Anne Blincoe, a New York State folklorist who helped in the initial training of volunteers; Harvey Green, then social historian with the Margaret Woodbury Strong Museum in Rochester; Jonathan Holstein, quilt historian and curator of the Whitney Quilt Show in 1971; Laurel Horton, folklorist, consultant to other state quilt projects, and director of the South Carolina project; Cyril I. Nelson, senior editor at Dutton Studio Books and a quilt collector of long standing; Patsy Orlofsky, textile conservator; Elizabeth V. Warren, then curator of collections at the Museum of American Folk Art; Judith Reiter Weissman, quilt historian with special emphasis on women's history; and Shelly Zegart, quilt dealer and historian, and the "mother" of state quilt projects.

During the planning stages, photographers were interviewed, questionnaires of other state projects were reviewed, museum collections in the metropolitan area were visited, and as many interested quilters and needleworkers as possible were consulted, all in an effort

3. Recording the personal history of the quiltmaker and the quilt at a quilt documentation day. (Courtesy New York Quilt Project)

4. Volunteers hanging quilt in anticipation of visual recording at a quilt documentation day. (Courtesy New York Quilt Project)

to focus the inquiry on the best structure to use for field work and scholarly research.

The questionnaire was the result of much consultation. Laurel Horton and Lee Kogan, Assistant Director of the Folk Art Institute and Research Coordinator for the Project, spent many hours refining it so that it could elicit enough information without posing a hardship on the documentors or interviewees. It also had to serve the dual purpose of creating a data base that would eventually be computerized for archival storage.

It was decided that the best way to find quilts would be to hold public Quilt Days throughout the state so that quilt owners could bring their quilts in for photography and documentation. In return, they received valuable information about conservation and preservation. Realizing that many quilt owners would not be able to appear personally with their quilts at a Quilt Day, outreach attempts were made through publications catering to quilt owners, quilt and antiques collectors, and persons interested in collateral textile fields. Thus, quilts were documented and registered by mail, many from other states where New York State quilts had migrated. We wished to be as inclusive as possible in order to amass sufficient data to draw conclusions and understandings of the significance of quilts and quiltmaking in New York State.

Consulting the book by Lisa Turner Oshins, *Quilt Collections: A Directory for the United States and Canada* (Washington, D.C.: Acropolis Books, 1987), helped us to identify institutions that might have quilts made in New York State. Curators of those institutions who confirmed that there were New York made quilts in their collections were sent questionnaires. Dealers known for fine inventories and quilt collectors were also contacted.

The definition of a quilt being a textile sandwich with a top, batting, and lining, either stitched together or tied was the only prerogative stated for documenting a piece brought to us. However, from the very first Quilt Day, people appeared with unquilted tops and/or blocks that apparently had been intended to become quilts. Realizing that these pieces could yield information that would be useful in research, we accepted them. No individual judgment about artistic merit was made at the time of documentation.

Forty-five Quilt Days were held throughout the state over a period of twenty-one months. Deciding about where to hold Quilt Days depended partially on the availability of space and volunteers to do the intake, and our original planning aimed for complete county coverage. Although it was not possible for every one of the sixty-two New York counties to be visited, all the geographical regions of the state were well represented in the course of the Quilt Days. Grass-roots participation was encouraged by the Museum through an extensive network of volunteers from quilt guilds, homemaker councils, and cooperative extensions around the state. Area or regional coordinators from various quilt guilds became active volunteers in the cause, and they mobilized their members to become registrars, documentors, quilt hangers, and photographers for the Quilt Days. They were instrumental in locating space, obtaining local publicity, and arranging schedules. Quilt Days were held in churches, in Cornell Co-Op Extension offices, in local school cafeterias, in gyms and libraries, state and private university premises, in a YMCA, on a county fairground, in a museum, in a senior-citizens' center, in historical societies, and even at a public television station.

Approximately 6,000 quilts have been documented, including unquilted tops and blocks, and quilts are still being documented at the time of the publication of this book. The New York Quilt Project archive remains open, and we anticipate the ongoing documentation of New York State quilts.

We originally chose the pattern called New York Beauty for the logo of the New York Quilt Project for obvious reasons. We thought that we would be able to research the pattern and discover more of its elusive history. However, as we continued with our Quilt Days, New York Beauty quilts failed to appear with any frequency. In fact, very few were seen! One, which had been donated to the Oysterponds Historical Society, came only with the name of the donor, a family that summered in Orient, Long Island, and it cannot be stated with certainty that the quilt was made in New York State. The Society is trying to track the family history for further clues as to its origin. Another New York Beauty, made in New York State, was sent as a gift to Tennessee after the Civil War and surfaced there during the Tennessee quilt project. The story of that

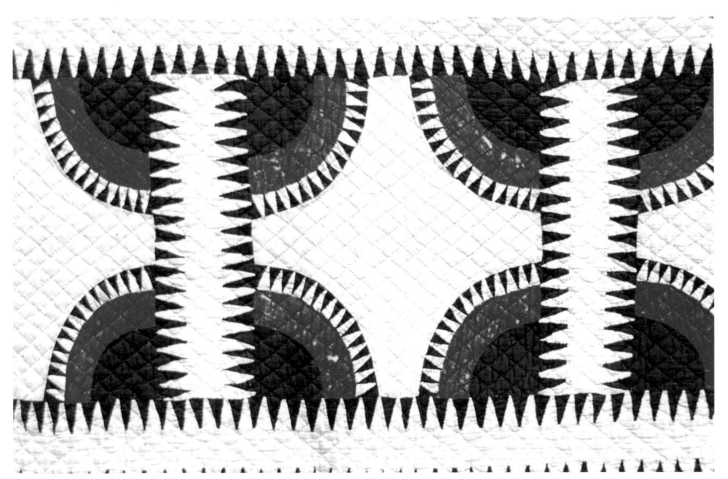

5. Detail of New York Beauty; maker unknown; New York State; 1865–1870; pieced cotton. Photograph courtesy *The Quilts of Tennessee.* (Collection of Jeanne Gilmore Webb) According to family history, in 1862 or 1863, the present owner's grandmother, Mary Lavinia Edwards, and great-grandmother, Martha Jane Vaughan Edwards, discovered a wounded Union soldier hiding in a barn on their property near Fosterville, Tennessee. The men of the family were all in the Confederate Army, but these two compassionate women—who chose to ignore the fact that their action was treasonous—moved the soldier to the attic of their home and cared for him until he could return to his unit. When the war ended, the soldier's mother sent a quilt in appreciation of what the women did for her son. Mrs. Webb notes that as a child she recalled helping her mother to air quilts twice annually and that "we referred to this one as the 'Civil War Quilt.'"

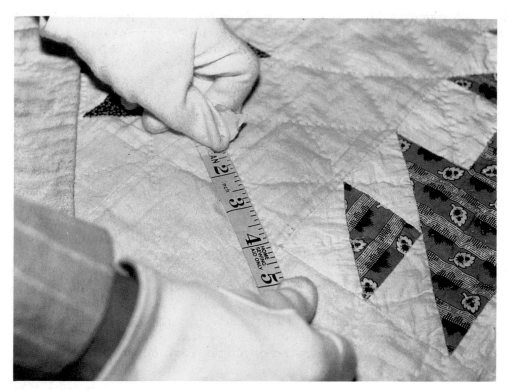

6. Measuring and recording the physical and technical details of a quilt during a quilt documentation day. (Courtesy New York Quilt Project)

quilt appears in our book. However, we have retained *New York Beauties* as the name for the book because we like it and also to point up the difficulties in finding when and how patterns originated and the names they were given either at their origin or at subsequent times. Inadvertently, the choosing of the name for this book demonstrates the need for documentation projects.

The popular notion that quilts were made solely for need is inconsistent with what has been documented by the New York Quilt Project. The quilts featured in this book were created with a strong sense of aesthetics as well as for the purpose of providing warmth. Quiltmakers took pride in their work, many times signing and dating their quilts. References to quilts in the writings of quiltmakers suggest an awareness of the desire to create an object of beauty. Earlier quiltmakers might have come to artistic solutions intuitively. With the advancement of women's education, more leisure time, and more visual stimulation through better communication and accessibility of magazines, quiltmakers seeking to make an object of beauty began to explore color relationships and invent new ways to improve on known designs.

In telling the story of the quilts, the social history of the state will be revealed in more human terms than that usually found in history texts. Louis Jones stated the case for social history when he wrote, "The past should have as many personal ties for each of us as possible, for none should feel that he is floating in time, rootless and unrelated to all that has happened to our fathers and to those who lived in our place before us....In the framework of the home let there be hand-me-downs from yesterday—pictures and furniture or a piece of lace...things that have been in a family a long time have a magic of their own, asserting the values of life and its survival."[1] Quilts are both documents of history and witness to the lives of ordinary beings. Written across their surfaces are stories of personal relationships within families and communities. With each passing generation the changes in family life, local lore and customs, politics, religious movements, and economic systems take us farther away from our roots. With the passage of time, many of the finest and earliest examples of quilts are lost to us and with their loss, our connections to the past suffer and we are diminished.

Because this is a social history of New York State as seen through the quilts made by its citizens, we have tried to relate the quilts to various historical events as they occurred. However, we found that there were many connections that could be made for an individual quilt that had more than one context in which it could be portrayed. A case in point is the quilt made by the ladies of Miller Place, Long Island, illustrated on page 78. It has ties to education, social history, and religion, as well as to fabric and design elements specific to a particular period in quiltmaking, so that it could have been placed in the text to illustrate any one of a number of subjects. The format of this book is not haphazard, and where a quilt has more than one context in which it may be considered, cross references will appear.

There were many criteria that could have been used for the selection of quilts to be illustrated here. Marsha MacDowell, the folklorist who conducted the Michigan Quilt Project, has noted that, "The development of an aesthetic theory as a foundation for survey and research projects...is critical to their success."[2] The New York Quilt Project is an art museum's undertaking with a mandate to discover the unique art of the quilt as well as social and individual history. The visual impact of a quilt as art was the primary consideration for inclusion in this book. It was no easy process to select from the 6,000 or so quilts tabulated during the Quilt Days those that would be the finest aesthetically and at the same time be representative of the quilts made throughout the state. Many quilts that were worthy of being in the book were not available to us for reasons known only to their owners.

There is considerable intellectual disagreement among the art-history establishment and folklorists. With many of the state documentation projects now coming to fruition and publication, there is dissent as to the validity of using state boundaries as a determinant in quilt documentation. Yet state boundaries were very often determined by geography, a fact attested to by the continual border problems in the early history of the state. Geography plays an important role since things are the way they are because of their location. Using state boundaries, which are political contrivances, as determining parameters is a convenience necessary to help organize the enormous amount of material collected and should not summarily be dismissed as unsound.

The Museum of American Folk Art has tried to reconcile the issue by considering artistic expression within a cultural context. The methodology used, and parameters as to how many and which quilts should be included, may come in for criticism, but to paraphrase an ancient Chinese scholar, if we waited for absolute perfection, this book would never have been finished. We feel that the New York Quilt Project has done justice to the people and quilts of the state and that a firm foundation has been set for continuing research. As Dr. Robert Bishop aptly stated in his foreword, "This book is the ongoing progress report of the work of the New York Quilt Project...."

PHYLLIS A. TEPPER
Director of the New York Quilt Project

7. Detail of Mariner's Compass; thought to have been made by Margaret Charlesworth (1826–1906); Avoca, Steuben County; mid nineteenth century; pieced and appliquéd cotton. (Collection of Jeanne Townsend)

Images of the Past
NEW YORK STATE REFLECTED IN ITS QUILTS

New York State is endowed with a prime geographic location on the eastern seaboard that allows easy access to its natural harbors and inland waterways and with abundant natural resources that encouraged settlement and commerce. From its earliest days, the state attracted a diverse population, created a multi-economic prosperity, and promoted cultural and educational institutions that, together, provide a rich social history. The quilts of the state, made by women and men of varied ethnic and national heritage, from a range of economic classes, and with stories as diverse as the fabrics they used, add texture and common threads to the story of New York.

More than 5,000 years ago, bands of people migrated southeasterly from the northernmost reaches of the North American continent. The dense forests and navigable rivers of what is now New York State attracted settlements by two major Native American groups, the Algonquins and related tribes, about the year 1000, and the Iroquois, comprising several tribes, about the year 1300. Villages, with a structured society and a division of labor, were formed in these eastern forests to create a hospitable and less isolated environment. With the arrival of the Europeans in the early seventeenth century (both the Dutch and the French had outposts as early as 1609), the geographic area that was to become New York State became one of the earliest European settlements on the eastern seacoast, and the synthesis that occurred from the resulting interaction of alien cultures had lasting political, economic, and social effects on the development of the state.

The Hudson River was first discovered in 1609 by Henry Hudson, an Englishman, who sold his claim to the Dutch. In 1614, the Netherlands granted a patent to several merchants for exclusive trade on the river. This group sent a heterogeneous group of settlers to New Netherland, as the territory was then called, including French-speaking Protestants, Dutch Calvinists, British subjects, and some Germans, Finns, and Jews. A small group of Swedes settled along the Delaware River, and blacks from Brazil and Angola were brought in as slaves. In 1644, Governor William Kieft remarked that "eighteen languages were spoken at or near Fort Amsterdam [now

New York City]."[1] Settling in the Hudson Valley as far west as the Mohawk and Delaware Rivers, as far east as Long Island, and as far south as what is now New Jersey, the immigrants found good farm land, a temperate climate, excellent waterways for transportation, and one of the finest natural harbors in the country at the mouth of the Hudson River.

Shortly after the arrival of the Dutch, small parties from the New England colonies began to arrive on the marshy necks of land along the north and south shores of eastern Long Island, where they were tolerated by the Dutch who had already settled the western sections. This group carried within their collective memories their English heritage, including social attitudes, skills, aesthetic tastes, and their religion.

In the earliest years of settlement, both English and Dutch coexisted with the Indians, who already lived on the land, but relations were gradually strained as the newcomers' thirst for land increased, and the Indians were slowly forced into other areas, leaving the Dutch and English to fight with each other for control. This situation was perhaps exacerbated by the fact that Charles II had granted the Connecticut colony a charter extending its title from ocean to ocean, while New Netherland regarded its boundaries as running from the Delaware River to Cape Cod.[2] Thus, the territory that was New York changed hands from Dutch to British and back again over the next fifty or so years, finally remaining in British hands from about 1674 until the Revolutionary War. In spite of the revolving national affiliations, one early historical account noted that, "very few of the [Dutch] inhabitants thought proper to remove out of the country; and their numerous descendants are still in many parts of this state and New Jersey."[3]

The Dutch domination in New York State's earliest years set a pattern and implanted certain traditions and characteristics that still persist today: "a commercial spirit, a keen interest in material things, a zest for life, and a tolerance towards people of varying religions and racial backgrounds."[4] Geographic place names such as Kinderhook, Harlem, Brooklyn, Rotterdam, and Amsterdam; common nouns such as boss, stoop, and cruller;

8. Whole Cloth; made by Eve Van Cortlandt (1737–1836); Bronx County; 1760; linen, 97¾″ x 86½″. (Collection of Smithsonian Institution, Washington, D.C.) This fine white linen quilt was made by Eve Van Cortlandt, the sixth child of Frederick and Frances Van Cortlandt. Her initials "EVC" and the date 1760 are cross-stitched in blue silk on the lining of the quilt. She was born and baptized "op de Manor" (at the manor), the family home that is now part of lower Yonkers and is presently maintained by the National Society of Colonial Dames. Eve married Henry White, Sr., a member of His Majesty's Council for the Province of New York, President of the Chamber of Commerce of New York (1772–1773), and a wealthy merchant. White was a loyalist and retired to England after the Revolutionary War. He died in London in 1786 and his widow returned to New York to live. She left a will in which she bequeathed her wearing apparel and household and other "linnen" to her daughters, Margaret and Frances, to be divided equally between them. She left annuities to three free blacks who had formerly been her slaves, and also to Sarah, a free mulatto (formerly her slave), who continued to live in England, and gave instructions "to pay to Hannah, a free black woman who lives with me and who was formerly my slave an annuity of fifty two dollars fifty cents like money annually in half yearly payments during her natural life, provided the said Hannah shall live with me to my death, or shall have left my service with my entire approbation and consent."

9. Portrait of Eve Van Cortlandt by an unknown artist, early nineteenth century, oil on canvas. (Courtesy Van Cortlandt House: The National Society of Colonial Dames in the State of New York)

other colony suffered from the border wars of the Revolution as did New York and, within that colony, the greatest sufferers were the valleys of the Schoharie and the Mohawk."[5] This region, with its fertile farmland (the Schoharie Valley alone supplied the patriot army with 80,000 bushels of wheat during the war), its heavily populated frontier outposts, and its closeness to Albany, made it a prime target for the British as they moved down

and many distinguished family names such as Roosevelt and Van Buren are a continuing legacy. Two lovely whitework quilts also add their reminder of the Dutch legacy to the state, of traditions that have persisted through the years.

During the first half of the eighteenth century, Palatine Germans arrived in the state, settling first in the mid-Hudson Valley, then moving north and west into the Schoharie and Mohawk Valleys. New Englanders continued to move across the Connecticut and Massachusetts borders into southern Dutchess and Westchester Counties. Twenty-five years prior to the Revolutionary War the pace of settlement quickened. The treaty following the French and Indian wars forced the French to pull back to Canada and relinquish the lands they held in the Hudson Valley north of Albany; it also pushed American Indians beyond the European settlement area, and New Englanders were quick to seize the opportunity to move into the lands vacated by the Indians as well as into the upper Susquehanna Basin, where they were joined by Scotch-Irish immigrants.

By 1775, the colony of New York had a population of about 200,000, concentrated primarily near the Hudson River and along the coastal areas of the Atlantic Ocean and Long Island Sound. Although many different nationalities were represented, those of Dutch and English background remained dominant both in population and influence.

New York played a major role in the War of Independence and in the establishment of the nation immediately thereafter. Fathers, husbands, brothers, and lovers of many New York quiltmakers went off to war, some never to return again. The early part of the war saw some military disasters within the state: the battle of Long Island was lost by the revolutionary forces, and New York City was evacuated by Washington and his troops, while Tory sympathizers and Indian groups upstate contributed valuable aid to the British. One writer stated that, "No

10. Whitework cradle quilt; made by Sarah Varick Hewlett; New York; c. 1830; cotton; 64½" x 49". Photograph by Mark Gulezian. (Collection of DAR Museum, Washington, D.C.; Gift of Helen W. Jones) The stuffed and embroidered work on this quilt was unmatched among the whitework pieces seen during the course of the Project. In addition to the excellence of its work, the quilt is unusual among whitework pieces in that it was put together in blocks and rectangles rather than being a whole-cloth piece. Although the quilt dates from about 1830, it is worked in a very traditional Dutch style of stuffed work overlaid with embroidery that is known as "zaam stickwerke," which is typical of work done near the Zaam River in the Netherlands. The quiltmaker, Sarah Varick Hewlett, was of Dutch lineage, and it is possible that the skills exhibited in the extraordinary work on this quilt had been preserved and handed down in her family from Dutch ancestors.

11. Tambour quilt; made by Mildred ———; Cos Cob, Rye, Westchester County; 1753; linen; 84″ x 78″. (Courtesy America Hurrah Antiques, New York City) This is the earliest dated quilt seen during the Project. Inscribed with beige linen thread in cross-stitch embroidery is "Mildred Cos Cob-Rhy 1753." When this quilt was made, state borders did not exist, and Colonial borders were nothing if not flexible. "Rhy"— or Rye—in present-day Westchester County, New York, and Cos Cob, in Connecticut, were neighboring communities, and closely intertwined economically and socially. Inasmuch as Mildred herself seemed to identify with both places, it was decided to accept a probable New York venue for the quilt, with a nod of appreciation to our neighboring state. This was one of the very few quilts in which tambour work was found. Combined with the block-printed borders quilted with indigo linen thread, it presents a living document of the fabrics and skills of the times. Tambour work, which is worked on a frame in the shape of a drum (from which the name is derived, tambour meaning drum in French), was known in China, Persia, India, and Turkey long before it became known in the West about the first quarter of the eighteenth century. Advertisements announcing the working or teaching of tambour work can be found in New York newspapers. For example: "Mrs. Cole from London, worker in Tambour and Embroidery, Has taken apartments at Mr. Matthew Ernest's opposite the Mr. Andrew Hammersley's near Coenties Market; where she works in Tambour ladies robes,...N.B. She teaches Ladies the Tambour Work expeditiously, and on the most reasonable terms." (From *The New-York Gazette and the Weekly Mercury*, September 6, 1773)

12a. Detail

12 and 12a. Crewel-embroidered quilt; made by Keturah Young (b. 1778); Aqueboque, Suffolk County; 1806; pieced and appliquéd linen and cotton; 93¼″ x 78″. Photograph by Mark Gulezian. (Collection of DAR Museum, Washington, D.C.; Given in memory of Helen H. Young) Keturah Young, daughter of the Revolutionary War soldier Nathan Young, inscribed her name and the date in cross-stitch on the face of this lovely early quilt. The eighteen crewel-embroidered appliqués stitched to a linen ground retain the fresh colors of natural dyes, and the block-printed cotton border complements the overall design of the quilt. Unlike English crewel designs, which often used exotic plant and animal designs, American crewel tended to portray everyday subjects, as Keturah does here in her depiction of birds, butterflies, and domestic animals. The use of the clamshell design in the quilting may also be a reflection of her locality, inasmuch as many Long Islanders have close ties to the sea.

from Canada in an effort to regain control of the Hudson Valley and its environs. The northern part of the state managed to stay free of British domination, but New York City remained under British control until the end of the war.

Once a constitution was ratified and a formal government established after the war, New York City—again by virtue of its geographical location and its increasing importance in commerce—became the first seat of the new government. The city did not cease to thrive after the government removed to Philadelphia, as its economic direction had been set and its position as a premier city of the new nation established.

Following the Revolutionary War, settlers spread westward to every part of the state that was habitable. Land speculation was rife, fortunes were made and lost, and many of today's real-estate patterns can be traced back to the original surveys and selections of sites that occurred at this time.[6] The speculation had one positive side effect—it made possible the rapid division and distribution of land to small individual proprietors and thus democratized the evolving economic and political system of the new nation.

Many of the incoming settlers during this period were from New England, where the available land supply was shrinking in comparison to population growth. The first national census in 1790 placed New York fifth among the states, with a total population of 340,120.[7] European immigration was minor, but in some localities, where large groups of foreigners settled, dominance by the migrating group transformed the cultural uniformity of some rural areas and smaller towns and villages into microcosms of cultural diversity. Such was the case in the Remsen district north of Utica, where Welsh immigrants retained their native language in the churches and newspapers for decades.

New York's history is the prototype for the traits we often label "the American way of life"—that is, a heterogeneous population, a diversified economic system marked by a strong entrepreneurial spirit, a high degree of urbanism, a pluralistic culture tolerating differences in social institutions, national backgrounds, and economic status, and a dynamism that, while preserving traditional values, has been a source of leadership in many fields of endeavor. George Washington saw the potential of New York State when traveling there in 1784 and aptly used the phrase "seat of empire." This was later corrupted by some unknown enthusiast to "The Empire State," and it has remained the state's official nickname ever since.

The growth of the state slowed somewhat after the turn of the century as problems with England continued to plague the new nation. Before the Revolutionary War, England had claimed the right to control the government, commerce, and revenue of the colonies; afterward she claimed the right to search American vessels for

13. Free Trade; made by Ann Eliza Sharts; Hillsdale, Columbia County; c. 1835; pieced cotton; 87½" x 70¼". (Collection of Margaret Woodbury Strong Museum, Rochester, N.Y.) This variation of the Free Trade patch has pieced lettering giving the maker's name and town running around three sides of the border. The concept of free trade was a factor in calling the Constitutional Convention of 1787. Under the earlier Articles of Confederation, tariffs imposed by the individual states created barriers to the production and distribution of less expensive fabrics throughout the states. Thus, the push for free trade was promoted by the desire to assure freedom from those internal barriers that were inhibiting full and open commerce among the states. This pattern is an example of political and economic events inspiring a quilt-block name.

"deserting" British seamen, a practice that led to the impressment in the British Navy of many American sailors. This, in conjunction with the sweeping blockades set up by the British to cut off supplies to France (with whom England was then at war)—thereby halting a lucrative American trade—was the impetus that sent the country back to war. A good portion of the War of 1812 was fought along the Canadian border, and New York saw a number of noteworthy engagements along the so-called Niagara frontier.[8] Nathaniel Harrington, the husband of the maker of one of the quilts registered, is known to have fought in the battle of Sackett's Harbor,

14. Mariner's Compass variation (Blazing Star); probably made by Mrs. James Strough; Herkimer, Herkimer County; c. 1840; pieced wool and linen; 70" x 70". Photograph by Mark Gulezian. (Collection of DAR Museum, Washington, D.C.; Gift of Mrs. Harry E. Boyd in memory of Edna Pierce Boyd and Harry E. Boyd) This simple variation of the Mariner's Compass pattern is unusual in that the top is made of wool. The weight and thickness of the fabric raise the possibility that it may have come from textiles used for military uniforms around the time of the War of 1812. It is not known whether the maker of the quilt had relatives who would have fought in that war or what other access there would have been to such textiles. The backing of the quilt is made from two different roller-printed linens that are compatible with the 1840 date.

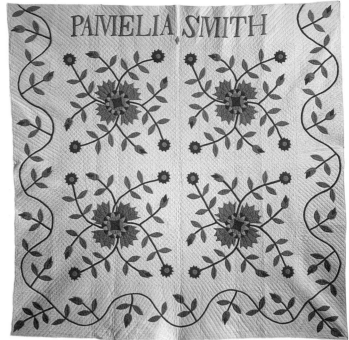

15. Whig Rose variation; probably made by Diana Edmunds Harrington (1789–1854); Rodman, Jefferson County; 1850; appliquéd cotton; 76½" x 74½". (Collection of Frances R. Harrington) This quilt continues to pose an intriguing mystery that has yet to be solved. It was inherited through Mrs. Harrington's late husband's family, and family lore says that it was made by Diana Edmunds Harrington in 1850, even though the name Pamelia A. Smith is appliquéd on the quilt. From family records and stories we know that Pamelia Smith (1785–1859) and Diana Harrington were apparently good friends, living near each other and attending the same church. It is not known whether the quilt was made by Diana for Pamelia as a gift, or how it came to remain in the Harrington family's possession rather than the Smiths'. It is possible that Pamelia actually made it and gave it to Diana (although it might be considered unusual for the donor to have given her name such prominence rather than that of the giftee), but there is no evidence to prove this. Neither Pamelia nor Diana had children or grandchildren named Pamelia, so it was unlikely to have been made as a wedding gift for one of them. Thus, the maker and the motivation continue to remain shrouded in the mists of time. The present owner lives in the original Harrington homestead and has portraits of Diana as well as other personal belongings such as her original quilt frames.

16. Diana Edmunds Harrington

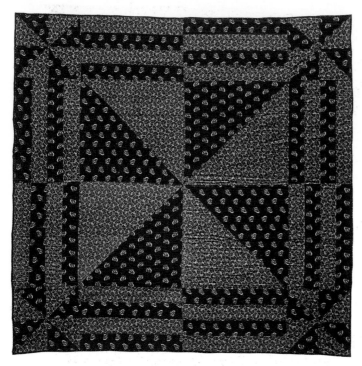

this utilitarian quilt, now owned by the maker's great-niece, was made from fabrics washed ashore from the *George Appold*, a steamer that had been wrecked on the night of January 8-9, 1889, in the waters off the eastern end of Long Island. Some enterprising citizens managed to profit from such disasters, and there were even those who speculated that some shipwrecks were not necessarily acts of nature but rather could be attributed to acts of man. The *Appold*'s cargo consisted of one hundred barrels of New England rum, a great quantity of "calico in ugly colors," coarse clothing, and heavy cheap shoes. Following the ship's foundering, "farm wagons came to Montauk from Amagansett and the nearby Hamptons to share in whatever might wash ashore. Thrifty mothers wore house dresses, aprons, and sunbonnets for years, made from a certain chocolate-brown calico with white rings on it, or another pattern in red and yellow, and made it into little girls' school dresses. Elderly women today recall with tears in their eyes how they loathed those dresses made of *Appold* calico....Bits of calico are still in evidence; it went into patchwork quilts when the dresses wore out."[1] One of the local papers reporting on the wreck had this comment to make: "The steamer *Appold*, on Montauk, has gone to pieces, and the beach is strewn with merchandise, such as calicos, boots and shoes, etc., and it is wonderful how many have suddenly gone into the dry or wet goods business in gathering up the find, and rumor says that they have been quite fortunate."[2]

17. Pinwheel; made by Mary Augusta King (1869–1968); Amagansett, Suffolk County; c. 1890; pieced cotton; 74″ x 74″. (Collection of Marilyn Stubelek) Ships and shipping have always been important to the economic life of New York State, but it was not without its hazards. According to family history,

---

[1] Jeannette E. Rattray, *Ship Ashore: A Record of Maritime Disasters off Montauk and Eastern Long Island 1640-1955* (New York: Coward McCann, 1955), 132-33.

[2] East Hampton Correspondence Column, *Sag Harbor Express*, January 24, 1889.

18. Painting by Mary Keys, *Lockport on the Erie Canal*, 1832; watercolor on paper. (Courtesy Munson-Williams-Proctor Institute, Utica, New York)

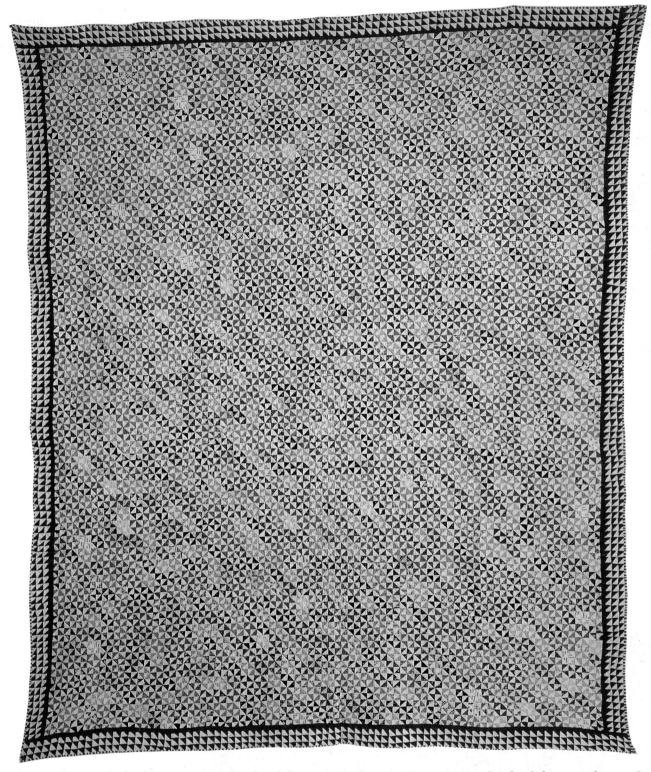

19. Broken Dishes; made by Nancy Armina Snyder Osborn (1817–1909) and Eva Van Loon Besemer; Tompkins County; 1850–1875; pieced cotton; 101½″ x 84″. (Collection of Carl English) This spectacular quilt contains over 21,000 pieces, the most of any quilt documented during the course of the Project. Mrs. Osborn, the wife of an Erie Canal barge captain, apparently got some help from her mother, Eva Van Loon, during the time it took to assemble the 21,559 postage-stamp-sized pieces. Nancy Armina Snyder Osborn was born at Snyder Hill, near Besemer, east of Ithaca. When her husband retired from his job on the canal, they made their home on a piece of land bought from her father. Her grandfather was one of the first settlers in the region—in 1802, still wilderness—and came from Essex County, New Jersey. According to family tradition, the quilt is passed down to the oldest male in each generation.

and it is said that his wife, Diana, molded the bullets that he used in this fight. In September of 1814 a stirring battle at Plattsburgh, New York—which ended in victory for the Americans—put an end to the fighting on the northern frontier, although it was not until the end of the year that a peace treaty was finally signed.[9]

Between the British blockade during the war and an American embargo put into place in retaliation, American sea-going commerce suffered greatly, and the rest of the country felt the repercussions in a widespread economic depression. The war did serve, however, to point up the need for less reliance on foreign-made goods and spurred manufacturing efforts, especially textiles. It also served, in view of the expanding American frontiers and the concomitant population migration, as a much-needed vehicle for national unification.

As the effects of the war years receded, the state's economy again gained ground. Shipping had always been tremendously important to the economy of the state, and New York City, with its central location and fine harbor, was one of the most active seaports along the east coast. Trade, both national and international, flourished, and ships from ports around the world wended their ways to New York to take advantage of the thriving markets for goods offered by the young nation.

Both shipping and the economy of the state were further enhanced in the ensuing years, first by the building of the Erie Canal and later by the spread of the railroad. The opening of the Canal in 1825, after years of planning and hard work, proved to be one of the most significant features in making New York "The Empire State." It also had far-reaching national import, for the Canal, along with its later lateral system of canals (many of which were used to carry European emigrants to their new homes) bonded the eastern with what was then the western part of the country by linking New York City with the Great Lakes. The Canal is viewed as the single most important unifying force that helped shape the state into one economic unit—indeed, a "pathway to empire."[10]

The opening of the Canal meant that it no longer took up to six weeks to travel between Buffalo and New York City, and the former isolation of many rural communities began to disappear as people and goods started to move much more freely and easily around the state. The Canal significantly cut the costs of doing business, which also helped to stimulate manufacturing growth. This economic boom boosted land values along the Canal and set the course for some villages, such as Rochester, Syracuse, and Buffalo, to become major cities within the state.

The Canal gave employment to many people. Some made their livelihoods from the produce and merchandise that floated along these gentle highways, while others depended heavily on access to these goods for providing a quality of life beyond the realm of the bare necessities. Hundreds, if not thousands, of men were part of the extensive support system necessary for operating and maintaining the canal locks and adjoining towpaths. Many of the canal barges that plied the waters of the three hundred-plus miles of the Canal were owned by their captains, who often had their families living with them aboard the barges. Among those who lived on the canal and earned income from it was the husband of quiltmaker Nancy Osborn, maker of a vibrant Broken Dishes quilt registered during the project. Captain Osborn piloted a canal barge between the central New York region and New York City, and his wife regularly traveled with him. They would bring produce from the rural agricultural areas to the city markets; the trip took from three to four days each way, thus allowing many hours for quiltmaking.

Railroads in New York initially were seen as a supplement to the canal system, but by the mid-century mark they had become an important transportation feature in their own right. As they increased in size, establishing both intrastate and interstate connections, they began to compete with the Erie Canal for business. Buffalo was connected to New York City by a nearly completed double track system by 1863; the cities were also connected through their own telegraph line. The railroad not only provided a more rapid mode of transportation than the canal barges, it also reached into places where the canal system could not go and, in so doing, altered agriculture, trade, manufacturing, and population trends in the state.

The rate of population growth in the state kept pace with that of the nation. From 1825 to 1855 there was

20. Canals, railroads, and roads. (Courtesy John Jackson Glass Negative Collection) Railroad tracks and a road run alongside the Erie Canal, pointing up New York's development of excellent transportation facilities that contributed to the diverse economy of the state.

21. LeMoyne Star; made by Elizabeth Clark (1806–1889); North Argyle, Saratoga County; c. 1837; pieced cotton; 100″ x 85″. (Collection of Catherine Craw) This quilt holds poignant memories for the present owner. Her great-grandmother was raised as a foster child by the quiltmaker, Elizabeth Clark, after her own mother died following her birth. The quilt was made as a gift for the motherless child and it included fabric from a dress of her natural mother (the brown fabric in the stars). Elizabeth Clark was born in Ireland; after coming to America, she married John Clark, owner of a store in North Argyle, who helped Irish people emigrating to this country.

22. Patriotic; made by Mary C. Nelson; Saratoga County; 1846; appliquéd cotton; 72¾″ x 87¾″. (Collection of Smithsonian Institution, Washington, D.C.; Gift of Miss Annie Pine) Twenty-eight stars surround the eagle on this quilt, and the twenty-eighth star is supposed to represent Texas, which joined the Union the year this quilt was finished. The eagle and the stars are made of discharge and roller-printed fabrics. The name of the quiltmaker and the year of completion are cross-stitched below the eagle on this quilt, along with the number 22, although whether this is the maker's age or has some other significance is not known. What is known is that Mary Nelson married Platt S. Pine and moved to his home in Sandy Plains, Greene County, New York. The donor of the quilt was a granddaughter of Mary Nelson.

23. Washington with Eagles; made by C.C. Shufelt; Hillsdale, Columbia County; 1853; pieced and appliquéd cotton; dimensions unknown. Photograph courtesy Davida Deutsch. (Private collection) This signed and dated quilt is a duplicate of one that was made in 1849 by Eliza Conklin of Claverack, also in Columbia County, that is illustrated in Myron and Patsy Orlofsky's *Quilts in America* and in Florence Peto's *American Quilts and Coverlets*. This would seem to indicate either that a body of similar work was being done in the region or that Christina Shufelt had seen the Conklin quilt and been enough taken by it to copy the design precisely. Although Peto (p. 30) notes that "at any threat to the Union…quiltmakers with intense loyalty patched and stitched the patriotic motif to show where they stood," this does not seem to hold for these quilts, for the Mexican War was over, and the Civil War was only a vague cloud on the horizon.

18

a slackening of immigration from native-born New Englanders, although Yankee stock remained the largest single ethnic group in the state throughout the nineteenth century. The black population grew slowly and, at this time, was actually lower than it had been during colonial times.[11] Emigration from Europe had begun to increase again, and by 1855 more than one-fourth of the state's population was foreign-born. Ninety percent of the state's foreign-born prior to the Civil War were from western and northern Europe, mostly from Ireland and Germany (the Irish in New York City constituted the largest Irish community in the world outside of Dublin). Scotch, English, and Welsh migrated to New York as well, but in smaller numbers, and an even smaller number of emigrants arrived from Scandinavia, Switzerland, and the Netherlands. This varied ethnic origin for the people of New York State was clearly seen in the family histories of the quilts reviewed, for nearly all nationalities were represented in those backgrounds.

With so much foreign immigration into the state, there were bound to be great antagonisms among various ethnic groups, and these were reflected most strongly in the Astor Place Riot in New York City. The stage was set starting in 1844 and 1845, when the Native Sons of America, the American Brotherhood, and the Native American Party (not to be confused with today's usage of Native American as an alternative for American Indian) were created by nativist fanatics who feared any and all foreigners and whose motto was "America for the Americans." This tinderbox situation, created by the forces of social unrest and unbridled jingoism (one of the ringleaders of the movement was E. Z. C. Judson, a political propagandist and writer better known as Ned Buntline), burst into flame in a riot at the Astor Place Opera House, sparked by the antagonism between two actors, William Macready, who was English, and Edwin Forrest, an American. Caleb Smith Woodhull, elected mayor of the city on May 8, 1849, had been in office for only two days when he was faced with the riot. Although military advisers felt that an early display of firepower would quell it, Woodhull refused to give the order and instead quit the scene, leaving the decision to others. Before the mob, estimated at 10,000 to 24,000 strong, was subdued, 150 people were wounded and 31 were killed.[12] The sister-in-law of Mayor Woodhull was a maker and signer of one quilt documented during the project (see page 65).

Religion also played a part in the antagonism toward immigrants. An atmosphere of religious tolerance had existed in New York in its early days, and many groups seeking religious freedom had found a home in the state, which eventually saw the establishment of representative congregations of a wide variety of religious groups. However, most of these early sects had been based in

24. Detail of Garden of Eden; made by Olive Newton Sheffer (1846–1918); Mechanicsville, Saratoga County; date unknown; pieced and appliquéd cotton. The complete quilt is illustrated on page 90. (Collection of Carol L. Mackay)

Protestantism, while many of the newer immigrants, particularly the Irish, were Catholic; thus the prejudice of the 1840s was as much attributable to a Protestant/ Catholic conflict of ideologies as to the pressure the immigrants placed on the job market that nativists regarded as their own.

Religion had always been an important factor in the lives of eighteenth- and nineteenth-century Americans, and this is clearly reflected in the many quilts seen with religious references of one sort or another, from simple presentations of pious sayings to elaborate depictions of biblical stories to patterns with names inspired by religious passages. Some quilts documented were made by members of well-known sects; others represented the hard work of serious church-going women who used their skills to honor their church leaders or to raise money for church coffers.

During the first half of the nineteenth century the New Englanders who came into the state looking for opportunity brought with them some of the religious ferment that had begun earlier in New England with the

25. Noah's Ark; made by Mrs. L. Converse; Woodville, Jefferson County; 1853; cotton; 87″ x 81″. (Courtesy America Hurrah Antiques, New York City) This quite extraordinary interpretation of the story of Noah and the Ark has been carefully researched by Sandi Fox in her book *Wrapped in Glory* (1990). She notes that the 1850 census shows two Converse families living in the Woodville area, both with women whose first names started with an L. Lydia Converse, sixty-five years old at the time of the census, and her husband, Thomas, lived with their youngest son, James, who was a successful farmer. While it is possible that she could have made the quilt, it is unlikely that at the age of sixty-eight she would have had the keen eyesight and steady hand required to execute the delightful inked drawings and text that lend this quilt its unique qualities.

The other Converse in the area, Rufus, was probably the brother of James (both men were listed as having been born in Oneida, New York). Rufus's wife was named Lutheria Converse and listed as L. Converse in the 1855 state census. She would have been thirty-two years old at the date given on the quilt, and Fox believes that it is more likely to have been her work rather than that of her mother-in-law.

26. Delectable Mountains; possibly made by Hepzibah Prentice; Alexander, Genesee County; 1848–1850; pieced and appliquéd cotton; 84″ x 81″. (Collection of Buffalo and Erie County Historical Society, Buffalo, N.Y.; Gift of Mrs. Julia Boyer Reinstein) This quilt shows a variation of the pattern known as Delectable Mountains. It was acquired by the Buffalo and Erie County Historical Society when they accessioned the fine quilt collection of Julia Reinstein. Reinstein had bought the quilt at an auction of the quilts owned by Jessie Farrell Peck, another well-known New York collector. The quiltmaker is thought to be Hepzibah Prentice of Alexander, Genesee County, and research on the maker is now in process. The cut-out corners indicate that the quilt was made to fit around the posts of a four-poster bed.

Second Great Awakening and the spread of Methodism. From 1825 to 1860 the expansion of Christian religious sentiment led by Charles Finney (sometimes called the father of modern revivalism) and other revivalists gained popularity, particularly in upstate New York. The evangelical fervor of the period stimulated church membership as well as the formation of a number of variant denominations and sects throughout the Northeast, and New York served as home to many of these.

The state seemed especially hospitable to Christian communistic societies, and leaders of great power and intensity directed movements that gained many adherents. Communitarian societies such as the Shakers, led by Mother Ann Lee, had been established as early as 1776 in the Albany area, and in 1788 the Universal Friends led by Jemima Wilkinson founded the New Jerusalem in what is now Keuka Lake. Joseph Smith, experiencing divine

inspiration from the angel Moroni, dictated the Book of Mormon in Palmyra, New York, in 1826. (Mormonism was the most important sect originating in New York, although its later and most extensive development occurred outside the state's borders.) Members of the Amana Society, a German pietistic movement, emigrated from Germany in 1843 and settled for a period near Buffalo before moving on to a permanent community in the Midwest. William Miller preached that Christ would return to the world to usher in the millennium, and, for a brief period, the "Millerites" attracted a number of followers. Swedenborgianism combined a liberal religious doctrine with the new sociological ideas of the time and a claim to be able to communicate with the dead; it attracted some educated men to its ranks, including such prominent New Yorkers as William Cullen Bryant and Horace Greeley.

Among the most widely publicized and successful of the evangelical movements were the Perfectionists (better known as the Oneida Community), which, under the leadership of John Humphrey Noyes, came to the state in 1848 after being driven from Vermont because of its doctrine of complex marriage. Noyes, a former Congregational minister, and his followers adopted a constitution that renounced religious observances and called for the pooling of property and the practice of eugenics. By 1847, the Perfectionists were being denounced for their theories and practices; the threat of legal action forced the group to leave Putney, Vermont, and they moved to Oneida, New York, in 1848, where the full organization of what came to be known as the Oneida

27. Open-air revival meetings of the mid nineteenth century attracted many adherents. (Courtesy John Jackson Glass Negative Collection)

28. Sampler Album; made by members of the Perfectionist Community; Oneida, Oneida County; 1873; cotton; 89″ x 79½″. (Collection of Oneida Community Mansion House, Oneida, N.Y.) The story of this quilt is told in the "Oneida Community Circular" of March 21, 1873. Many of the designs in the quilt symbolize the roles and occupations of community members. By reading each block in the quilt an accurate picture emerges as to the variety of life sustained by the community—industrial, financial, social, and cultural. The circular concludes that, "Those who used to be active at 'quilting' forty and fifty years ago, say they never heard of a quilt like this. It is an 'album bed quilt' with the wildest variations, and we imagine that half a century hence it will be an interesting memorial of the industries and aspirations of the year 1873."

Community occurred. The social organization of the Community was based on a number of advanced beliefs, of which complex marriage, where every woman was theoretically the wife of every man, was the most controversial.

The Oneida Community was one of the few communitarian societies that was an economic success. Through luck or planning, the 600 acres on which the members settled were fertile and highly productive. The Community developed the only successful silk-raising effort in the state, and sewing and embroidery silks were manufactured and sold. The production of silver-plated ware later became the Community's best-known and ultimately only product. The communal enterprise lasted until 1879, when Noyes, feeling that his advancing age might negate his leadership, proposed changes in the social organization of the community. The doctrine of complex marriage was given up and a change was made from communal ownership to a joint-stock corporation and private ownership of property.

The Mennonites also had a presence in southwestern New York State and probably had moved in from their earlier settlements in Pennsylvania and Ohio. (Mennonite is the general term for various religious sects, including the Amish, Hutterites, and other "plain people" sects, all of which have adopted various rules and regulations for governing their own communities.) From about 1870 on there had also been some Reformed Mennonite churches in that area, an offshoot of a conservative splinter group started in Pennsylvania around 1812. One such congregation was in Williamsville, New York (just outside of Clarence), as late as 1948, and several identified with the Mennonites have been documented from other parts of western New York.[13]

Humanitarian reforms were characteristic of the early to mid–nineteenth century and set the stage for the Empire State to take the national lead in public welfare provisions. Abolition of slavery, temperance, and support for legislation promoting social issues all provided platforms for religious concern during the century. There was also a great deal of Protestant missionary activity in the state through organizations such as missionary societies and Sunday schools. In fact, it has been said that the beginning of the new era in missionary activity can be dated from the formation of the New York Missionary Society in 1796, a joint project of Presbyterians, Baptists, and Dutch Reformed.[14] Although its primary object was the promotion of missionary work among Indians, it served as a model for other groups interested in establishing organized religion on the western frontiers of the country.

Fraternal orders served in a similar manner to religion to bond communities together, and the Masons were one such group that had a strong impact on the state's history. Such prominent politicians as Governor De Witt Clinton and Martin Van Buren were members of the group, and

29. Fleur de Lis signature quilt; maker unknown; Amherst, Erie County; 1849; appliquéd cotton; 83″ x 68″. (Collection of Warren H. Miller) This signature quilt was the product of a group of Mennonite women living in Erie County, and it is likely that it was made as a presentation gift, as a fundraiser, or both. The quilt was sold at an auction in 1962 of the estate of Mary Snearley, one of the twenty signers of the quilt, and purchased by the present owner's mother, a friend of the Snearley family. Mary Snearley was the daughter of one of the early ministers of the Reformed Mennonite Congregation, and it is possible that the quilt had been presented to her father. The present owner's grandmother was a Reformed Mennonite, as were the Snearleys, and the families were close. It is his belief that all the signers of the quilt were members of the Reformed Mennonites. This congregation was known to have strong ties to a similar group in Ontario, Canada, and one of the signers, a Barbara Millar, included "Canada" after her name.

the Masons became both an economic and political force. This changed radically, however, following an incident at Batavia, in western New York, in 1826. William Morgan wrote what purported to be an exposé of Masonic secret ritual and practices. When he disappeared without explanation, it was assumed by many that a Masonic group had done away with him in retribution for his breaking the vow of secrecy that is part of Masonic ritual. This created a wave of anti-Masonic actions that threatened political stability in the upstate area; it also

30. Prairie Star variation; maker unknown; Conewango, Chautauqua County; c. 1870; wool; 78″ x 78″. (Courtesy Laura Fisher/Antique Quilts & Americana, New York City) This unusual and striking quilt is a fanciful and remarkable design for a winter-weight woolen quilt. The palette and fabric are typical of Amish quilts, but the design is more inventive than what is usually found in an Amish quilt.

31. Original design (quilt top detail); made by Anne Bussing Thorburn (d. 1860); New York City or Brooklyn; first quarter of the nineteenth century; appliquéd cotton. (Collection of Mrs. John De Witt Cook) This wonderfully eccentric and finely appliquéd quilt top overflows with naturalistic images surrounding a central block full of Masonic symbols. No one knows why Anne Thorburn, who married James Thorburn on December 31, 1799, made the top, or what meaning it may have had, but it seems likely that there were Masonic ties either through her family or her husband's. The present owner is the daughter-in-law of the great-great-granddaughter of Anne Thorburn, and she plans to give the quilt to her daughter.

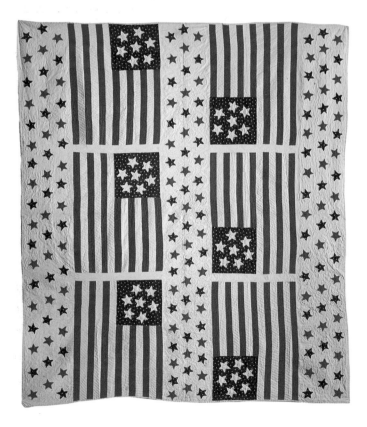

32. Original Patriotic; made by Anna Mariah Servoss Sweet (1839–1895); Montgomery County; c. 1858; pieced and appliquéd cotton; 102″ x 93″. (Previously in the collection of Oramay Lathers, Glen, N.Y., deceased; now in the collection of Audrey Hammond, Townville, S.C.) Anna Mariah Servoss married William A. Sweet on January 27, 1858; they had a farm in Montgomery County halfway between the towns of Fort Hunter and Minaville. According to the previous owner (granddaughter of the maker), the seven stars in the blue fields of the flags represent the seven northern states. Although New York was part of the Union during the Civil War and, for the most part, a staunch supporter, some areas of the state were not fully in favor of the Union cause and some residents, known as "copperheads," flew Confederate flags and even actively supported the Confederate cause. Perhaps this is the reason for the story that accompanies this quilt—family lore has it that the quilt was hidden during the Civil War so that it would not be found and destroyed.

reflected class differences between farmers and middle-class professional men, and many local government officials became tainted by innuendo and suspicion. The furor "swept over the western portion of the State...with the devastating power of a tornado. It...in some instances wholly broke up the social relations of life. [Masons'] names were thrown out of the jury box; and at the social gatherings of the grave matrons of the neighborhood resolutions were in many instances passed, forbidding their daughters keeping company with a Mason. The old party landmarks were thus swept away or swallowed up in this new element of discord and strife."[15]

By the time of the Civil War, freemasonry had regained its status as a respectable fraternal organization to which prominent businessmen, politicians, and clergymen belonged. It was primarily an organization of white Protestant men and by the late nineteenth century membership proved to be useful for personal connections. Membership in the Masons offered charity, trade, and political preferment, and opportunities for sociability to men anxious to be pillars of their local communities; it also offered a guarantee of acceptance when moving to a new community. Although women could not be members of the Masons, they could join the Order of the Eastern Star, a secret sororal organization for female relatives of Masons.[16] It allowed women to share, to some extent, their husbands' experiences of secrecy, ritual, and sociability.

Masonic symbolism lends itself to decoration and is, in itself, decorative. From early times, the adornments of official office, such as the aprons worn by members, as well as more personal objects related to ritual and membership have been painted, stitched, and bespangled. This strong decorative tradition is apparent in several quilts that were registered during the Project.

New York State, which had abolished slavery in 1824, was a hub of activity during the Civil War years. It provided the greatest number of soldiers to the Union Army, the greatest amount of supplies, and the largest amount of money. At the beginning of the war, the Union Army was a volunteer citizens' army, and many women were left to care for their children and themselves as best they could as their husbands, in a burst of enthusiasm for the Union and the expectation that the war would be won in a matter of weeks, joined as volunteers. As the months passed and it became clear that a rapid resolution to the conflict was a pipe dream, compulsory conscription was put into effect, which gave rise to a series of draft riots. These were not wholly protests against conscription but were bred in part by economic injustice—a man could find a substitute and buy his way out of service for $300, and so, almost by default, the burden of battle fell on newly arrived immigrants or men from the poorer economic groups who had no option but to serve. As the war dragged on and the numbers of dead and wounded daily grew larger, the price of a substitute rose to $1,000

33. Whig Rose; made by Marion Annette Weber Crandall (1827–1882); Nile, Allegany County; 1840s; appliquéd cotton; 78″ x 74″. (Collection of Marion Johnson) Marion Annette Weber married Samuel Park Crandall in 1843, when she was sixteen; the back of the quilt carries the initials M.A.C.–S.P.C. in cross-stitch, and family history relates that she made the quilt for her marriage, although no documentation exists to confirm this belief. Marion's father, Peter S. Weber, was quite active in the abolition movement. She lost two of her sons during the Civil War, one of them having been a prisoner at the infamous Andersonville Prison in Georgia. Of her four children, only one survived, her daughter Ellen Annette Crandall Irish, who was also a prolific quiltmaker. The present owner is a member of the fourth generation to have the quilt in her possession.

34. From the left: Peter S. Weber, Marion Annette Weber Crandall, and Samuel Park Crandall.

35. Log Cabin—Barn Raising design; made by Mary Jane Smith (1833–1869); Whitestone, Queens County; 1861–1865; pieced cotton, wool, and velvet; 81″ x 73¼″. (Collection of Museum of American Folk Art, New York City; Gift of Mary D. Bromham, grandniece of Mary Jane Smith, 1987.9.1) Mary Jane Smith was the daughter of John Smith and his wife, Mary Morrell Smith, prosperous farmers in Clintonville (now Whitestone), Queens County. She was engaged to a young man from Philadelphia who served in the Union Army and fought throughout the Civil War. While he was away, Mary Jane made an elaborate wedding trousseau, which included this quilt. At the end of the war, he established a home in Philadelphia, to which he intended to bring Mary Jane after their wedding. The prospective bride and her mother met the young man at his hotel in Manhattan the day before the ceremony was to take place but, soon after arriving back at their home, a messenger arrived to inform them that the fiancé had died of pneumonia shortly after they had left him. Mary Jane died three years later, and the quilt was never used. Mary D. Bromham, the former owner, is a grandniece of the quiltmaker.

and even $1,500; few but the wealthiest people could afford these tariffs, although there were towns that raised cash in an attempt to keep some of their menfolk at home.[17] There was also an active peace movement within the state during the war years, as well as pockets of Confederate support.

Although state politics were partially in turmoil for a good part of the war years, the New York home front prospered, even though there was speculation in the

markets on Wall Street and accusations of hoarding among merchants in order to run up prices. Transportation facilities and the textile trade expanded, and woolen manufacturers were said to have made enormous profits.[18] There was an increase in farm production, with women taking to the fields to gather the harvests in the absence of men.[19]

Shortages occurred as they do in any wartime. Housewives were urged to save their cotton rags, which could be sold and then recycled at the paper mills, and other wartime economies tied to textiles were also practiced. A weekly newspaper near the end of the war encouraged women to reuse old quilts as interior linings rather than to discard them and buy new cotton for batting, which was then hard to come by as well as expensive.[20] And Caroline Richards noted in a wartime entry in her diary that, "...grandmother told us [the sewing society] to save all the basting threads when we were through with them and tie them and wind them on a spool for use another time."[21]

That the war took its toll on the women of New York as well as the men they loved was evident in the stories attached to a number of the quilts seen on registration days. More than one woman occupied her time in stitching a quilt for her trousseau while waiting— sometimes in vain—for her man to return from war. One quilt was completed on April 4, 1865, the day the maker found out that her loved one had died as a result of war wounds; the quilt was put away, never to be used. Another, a top made by friends as a wedding gift, ended with the prospective bride's brown taffeta wedding dress being used as the backing after her fiancé was killed. Mary Jane Smith designed and made a stunning Log Cabin quilt for her trousseau while her fiancé was off at war; he survived the fighting only to succumb to pneumonia the day before their wedding, leaving an inconsolable bride-to-be who survived him by only three years.

New Yorkers actively participated in war bond drives and raised money for relief organizations. From Buffalo to New York City women developed organizations to care for wounded veterans and the needy dependents of soldiers. These efforts led to the establishment of the United States Sanitary Commission, which had its beginnings in New York City. Dr. Elizabeth Blackwell was the first woman in the United States to receive a medical degree. In 1861, she organized the Women's Central Association for Relief (WCAR), also known as the Women's Sanitary Commission, which created a training program for nurses and carried out relief activities. The war highlighted the desperate need for civilian services to back up the meager military medical services, and the WCAR, with its nucleus of trained women, formed a foundation on which a national Commission would be built.

Thousands of women volunteers made up its dedicated ranks and were responsible for raising the money that paid for the medicine, bandages, blankets, food, and nurses so urgently needed by the Union Army. One contemporary source noted that, "The women of the land could not follow those they loved in battle but, even before the smoke rolled away, they could help in binding up their wounds and ministering to them even though they were hundreds of miles away.... The women had enlisted for the war, and there was nothing intermittent or spasmodic about their labor. As long as the need lasted they were ready for service."[22]

Money was raised through Sanitary Fairs, some of which were held in New York. People contributed items that could be sold or auctioned to bring in the funds that would allow the Commission to carry out its work.[23] The April 1864 New York Metropolitan Fair, the largest of all the Sanitary Fairs, netted $1,200,000.[24] Although some of the items sent to the fairs were family heirlooms of one sort or another, more frequently they were the handiwork of the women who worked for war relief on the home front, and it was not unusual to find exquisite quilts among these contributions. No one knows for sure just how many quilts were made for all the Sanitary Fairs, but the New York branch of the Commission recorded a total of 26,408 quilts donated during the war years.[25] The Sanitary Commission provided an invaluable service to the Union during the war years, and, when the Red Cross was established in Geneva in 1864, it was widely acknowledged that the achievements of the Commission had provided inspiration to the group.[26]

Economically, the era after the conclusion of the Civil War was unstable for nearly ten years as the government sought to pull a war-torn economy back into working order. Veterans were offered free land in the western territories in lieu of pay owed them, and population in some areas of the state declined as men took advantage of the offer, gathered their families, and left to look for greater opportunities in the newly expanding frontier— the women taking with them tangible reminders of their former homes in the form of Friendship quilts. Probably the panic of 1873, in which many thousands became unemployed as companies and many small businesses went bankrupt, and the ensuing six-year depression pushed some of this movement to the West. By the end of the 1870s, however, the country had begun a return to economic vitality, most obvious in the renewed spurt in the growth of major cultural and social institutions that had been founded in New York City shortly after the Civil War. Life on the home front took an upswing for the better as well, and the predominantly rural lifestyle of the nation that had prevailed until prior to the war became more clearly urban in its orientation.

Until 1870, New York State's largest single occupational group was farmers, but, by 1880, the amount of land

36. Dutch Rose; made by Estella Ferris Witherhead (1867–1946); Oswegatchie, St. Lawrence County; late nineteenth century; pieced cotton; 93″ x 79″. (Collection of Mr. and Mrs. John M Taggart) The quiltmaker is the grandmother of John Taggart, the present owner. She was born in Millport, just north of Elmira, Chemung County, and her father was a color sergeant in the First New York Dragoons during the Civil War. She lived most of her life in the north country of New York State in Lisbon, Oswegatchie, and Ogdensburg. The family believes that she made this quilt while living in Oswegatchie.

under cultivation began to decline. Earlier farming had been of the subsistence type, where crops were produced for home consumption or for an exchange of goods, but now an expanded economy and technological change meant farms had to produce more to be economical. The Civil War had given a great impetus to manufacturing with its attendant labor needs, and jobs had become plentiful in the cities, drawing much-needed labor away from rural areas. Farms that had been marginal—where the soil, terrain, and climate were poor or were poorly located with respect to markets—and that had survived in large part because of the availability of cheap labor were abandoned in favor of better-paying jobs in the growing urban areas. The farmers that remained in New York turned from grain growing—so much more suited to the newly expanding farmlands of the Midwest—to dairy farming or some form of horticulture or truck farming.

37. Album; maker unknown; Dutchess County; 1870; appliquéd cotton; 84″ x 84″. (Collection of Audrey Martin) The quilt portrays some everyday scenes, including a milkmaid with her cow, probably a common sight in this era when dairy farms in New York were expanding. The present owner notes that the quilt descended in her husband's family and was made for a member of the Harris family. She does not know for sure whether the quilt was made by one or several makers, but because several names or initials are inscribed on different blocks, it is possible that more than one maker was involved. The equestrian figure has the name Mary J. Palmer inscribed below it. Variations on this elegant lady mounted sidesaddle on her horse have been seen in a number of album quilts and are probably a contemporary reflection of the high degree of interest in good horsemanship for women. *Miss Leslie's Magazine* notes in the November 1843 issue: "The practice of riding should be generally encouraged by parents. It will give a healthy tone to the constitution of their daughters, and make them more useful members of society than they ever can be by frequenting midnight dancing parties, and lolling on their couches during the day."

38. Martha and George Centennial; maker unknown; 1876; pieced cotton; 75½″ x 54¼″. (Photograph courtesy America Hurrah Antiques, New York City; Collection of Dan Brechner & Company) Printed yard goods commemorating the country's Centennial were plentiful and popular in 1876, and Centennial fabrics appeared in more than one quilt seen during the Quilt Days. This one, with a print depicting George and Martha Washington and the Centennial dates (1776–1876) stitched to satin-finish flag-printed cotton fabrics, was one of the more overtly patriotic quilts seen from that period.

39. Remember the *Maine*; made by Mary Dunne Leroy; Lakewood, Chautauqua County; c. 1898; pieced and appliquéd cotton; 70″ x 70″. (Photograph courtesy America Hurrah Antiques, New York City; Collection of Dan Brechner & Company) This quilt not only attests to the strong patriotic feelings of the quiltmaker but also is a document of the contemporary heroes who are now footnotes in American naval history. Dewey was the commodore in the United States Navy who sank eight ships of the Spanish fleet in Manila with a loss of only eight American sailors; Hobson was the naval officer who was responsible for sinking the collier *Merrimac* in the harbor of Santiago de Cuba, effectively blockading the port; and Sampson was the naval officer in charge of the inquiry into the destruction of the American ship *Maine*, as well as the commander who ordered the blockade of Cuba. "Remember the *Maine*" was, of course, the rallying cry of support for United States policy during the Spanish-American War.

40. Pan-American Exposition Commemorative; maker unknown; Buffalo, Erie County; 1901; pieced silk and velvet; 66″ x 80″. (Collection of James Francis) This commemorative quilt is composed of one-inch triangles in the silks and velvets favored by Victorian quilters. It was not finished as a quilt until two and a half years before its documentation in 1989. The present owner's mother, Marjorie Cummings, was the great-granddaughter of the maker; she had inherited the quilt and apparently stored it for eighty years in attics and basements. Mr. Francis, the owner, wished to use it as a wall hanging in his new home and so had it backed and quilted by the Sider Sisters of Fort Erie, Ontario.

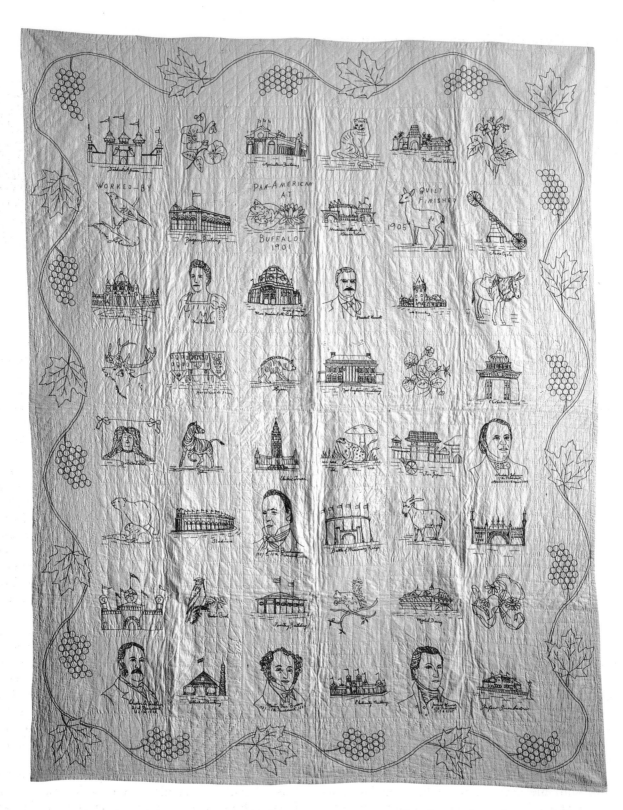

41. Pan-American Exposition (Penny Squares); made by Jennie Johnson; Niagara Falls area; 1901–1905; cotton, muslin; 80″ x 62″. (Collection of Susan Parrish Antiques, New York City) Jennie Johnson may have started this quilt to commemorate the Exposition, but it seems to be with some relief that she finally signed it with her name and "Quilt finished 1905"! The quilt, embroidered throughout with red cotton floss, is made in the "penny-square" style popular at the turn of the century. Jennie seems to have created some of her own designs, even though they are based on the standard blocks that could have been bought at the time. She also livened up the quilt as a whole with a graceful grapevine border, perhaps in tribute to some of the produce of her part of the state.

The days when the fertile Schoharie Valley was known as the "bread basket of the Revolution" were long gone as acreage once devoted to wheat and other grains was turned over to vegetables and fruit.

The patriotism that had grown rampant after the Civil War with the success of the Union cause continued to expand, culminating in the 1876 Centennial Exposition in Philadelphia, which unleashed a plethora of patriotic memorabilia on the country, including a large number of quilts with patriotic themes. This spirit spilled over to other parts of the world, and America continued to be seen as an opportunity for a better life, economically and socially. There were jobs to be had in the construction of roads, railroads, and canals. Religious freedom, individual political rights, and the ability to be upwardly mobile and cast off the class distinctions of the old world were added incentives to emigration.

The latter part of the nineteenth century not only saw a larger mix of nationalities within the country, it also saw the nation beginning to look outward at the larger international scene. Due to heavy investments of American businesses in Cuba, the strategic importance of that country to Latin America and the United States, and a growing sense of this country's power in the western hemisphere, it was only natural that Cuba's revolt against the arbitrary rule of Spain would be supported by the United States. American feelings against Spain were inflamed first by a letter published by William Randolph Hearst in which the Spanish minister in Washington wrote to a friend in Cuba expressing contempt for President McKinley, and later by the sinking of the battleship *Maine*. The ship had been sent to Havana at the request of the American consul, who feared harm to American nationals and property because of the growing unrest there. Less than a month after its arrival in Havana in 1898, a mysterious explosion sank the *Maine*, and 260 men were lost. An enraged American public blamed Spain for the tragedy, and "Remember the *Maine*" became the avenging patriotic slogan that was to feed United States patriotism. When President McKinley asked Congress for authority to intervene in Cuba, Congress responded affirmatively and a state of war was declared on April 21, 1898. In many ways, the Spanish-American War pushed the United States onto the world stage as the international policeman for maintaining the peace, although the war had little real impact on the life of New York State itself.

The turn of the century saw a continuing decline in agriculture, with the acres under cultivation lessening each year. The farm became subordinate to the factory, and the family farm as a self-contained economic unit began to lose its significance. Manufacturing continued to thrive within the state, and New York led the nation in the production of women's clothing at this time. It was also one of the country's leaders in printing and publishing, men's clothing, foundry and machine-shop products,

42. Teddy Roosevelt addressing the crowd at the Walton Fair. (Courtesy John Jackson Glass Negative Collection)

bakery and meat products, electrical machinery, motor vehicles, fur goods, and boots and shoes.[27] The ongoing industrialization greatly transformed daily life for everyone. The opening of the New York City subways in 1904 changed commuting life forever, and expanded rail and highway systems played an indispensable role in development of the more remote areas of the state and in the exploitation of its resources.

The Pan-American Exposition of 1901 in many ways symbolized the changing society. The Exposition, held in Buffalo and forever immortalized because of President McKinley's assassination there, was conceived of as the largest exposition this country had ever seen and was intended to be even larger than the World's Columbian Exposition held in Chicago in 1893. The name "Pan-American" was adopted to indicate its scope, and support was received from Congress and the New York State Legislature.

The planners thought big; twenty massive buildings to house the exhibits were to be built as well as a score of smaller ones. The style was intentionally Spanish-American in order to be expressive of all the Americas, and there was an emphasis on decoration rather than architectural effect. Within twenty months, a 350-acre farm was leased and canals, esplanades, outdoor sculptures, and fountains, in addition to the buildings, began to spring into life.

The Exposition, formally dedicated in May 1901 by Vice President Theodore Roosevelt, was a financial failure, although it had a lasting effect on Buffalo and the nation. Over 8,000,000 people walked in wonder through its impressive buildings and exhibits—which included Thomas A. Edison's wireless telegraph—and stood in awe of the 375-foot electric tower powered by the waters of Niagara Falls. Then, on September 6, 1901, President McKinley was assassinated while attending a public

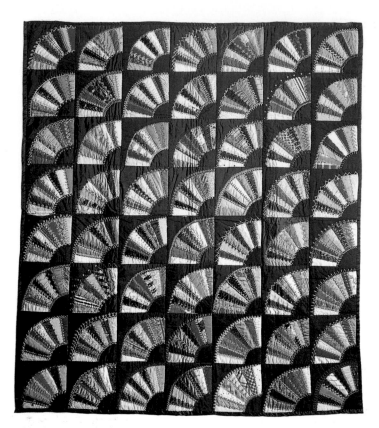

44. Lillian Russell, toast of the New York stage. (Collection of Laura Lopata)

43. Grandmother's Fan; made by Miss Hattie Whiting; New York City; c. 1900; pieced silk, velvet, satin, and brocade; 59″ x 66″. (Collection of Alice Hoppey) This striking quilt was made from scraps of fabric from costumes made for Lillian Russell, the famous turn-of-the-century actress, singer, and personality. The quiltmaker, Miss Hattie Whiting, was the wardrobe mistress to Miss Russell. She was one of three sisters; they belonged to the Methodist Church and were all accomplished seamstresses. Because of her work, Hattie lived mostly in New York City; her sisters frowned upon her life in the entertainment world, and she seldom went home to visit them in Matamoras, Pennsylvania. The mother of the present quilt owner was taken in as a foster child by the Whiting sisters, and it was Hattie who gave the quilt to her.

45. Women showed their patriotism by using their sewing skills to aid the Red Cross during World War I. (Courtesy John Jackson Glass Negative Collection)

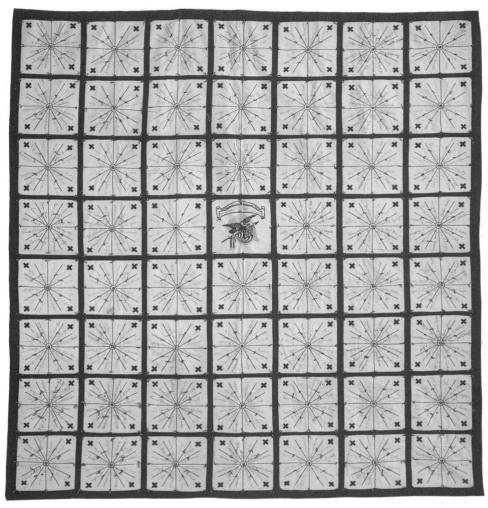

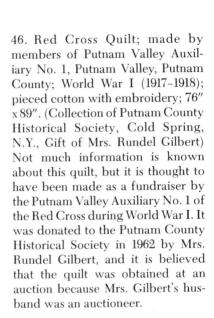

46. Red Cross Quilt; made by members of Putnam Valley Auxiliary No. 1, Putnam Valley, Putnam County; World War I (1917–1918); pieced cotton with embroidery; 76″ x 89″. (Collection of Putnam County Historical Society, Cold Spring, N.Y., Gift of Mrs. Rundel Gilbert) Not much information is known about this quilt, but it is thought to have been made as a fundraiser by the Putnam Valley Auxiliary No. 1 of the Red Cross during World War I. It was donated to the Putnam County Historical Society in 1962 by Mrs. Rundel Gilbert, and it is believed that the quilt was obtained at an auction because Mrs. Gilbert's husband was an auctioneer.

reception at the Exposition; the next day Theodore Roosevelt was sworn in.

The state continued to flourish from the turn of the century until World War I on almost all levels. The population continued to grow, although the growth was unevenly weighted toward the cities—by 1910 New York City had one-half the population of the state—and rural areas were losing their youth to the lure of the lights. Greater public education opportunities were available to all, and life on the cultural front expanded as well. New York City set the patterns and values in literature and art not only for the state but for the country as a whole. Most of the new art movements of the times started in New York; the most notable event of the era was the Armory Show of 1913, which established popular interest in modern art.

The theater—both drama and burlesque—had long been part of the city's heritage, and it also became a growing and important business enterprise for New York City. From the Civil War to World War I the popular stage in New York was distinguished by a kind of uninhibited

flamboyance that customers delighted in, and favorite performers were often elevated to stardom. Lillian Russell, for example, a great star of vaudeville, comic opera, and plays, was widely acclaimed at the turn of the century for her voice and beauty; it is said that "no other actress in the history of the New York stage ever so completely captivated male audiences over such a long period of time."[28] She was also indirectly responsible for one of the more elegant Fan quilts seen during the course of the project; made by her wardrobe mistress, the quilt is a jewel-like compendium of scraps from the elegant gowns—some from the famous Parisian designer, Worth—worn by Miss Russell in her shows.

The theater was not alone in its exuberance and imagination in the early part of this century. With technology leading to new frontiers in all parts of the media, New York became home to the pioneers in radio broadcasting, and, prior to the war, it also served as the center for the budding movie industry. All in all, times were good and the nation as a whole was unprepared for the impact of the "war to end all wars."

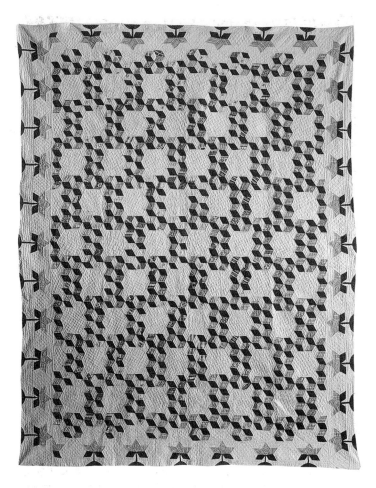

47. Tumbling Blocks in Stairway; made by Edith Ham Stickle (1888–1978); Red Hook, Dutchess County; 1919–1925; pieced cotton; 94″ x 73″. (Collection of Shirley Kane) The unusual handling of the traditional Tumbling Blocks pattern moves this quilt out of the realm of the strictly utilitarian. Edith Ham Stickle made the quilt when she was in her late twenties, and, according to her granddaughter who now owns the quilt, it is considered a unique pattern. The quiltmaker lived her entire life in Dutchess County, where her husband Edward made his living as a farmer and, in the winter, as an ice-cutter on the Hudson River. Along with raising her three children, she also did seasonal work as a greenhouse-worker in the spring and an apple-packer in the fall. During the Depression, the family had a four-generation household. Edith Stickle helped milk the cows and cut the hay fields, using horse-drawn machinery; she really liked this work and was happy to leave the housekeeping and cooking to her mother and married daughter.

48. Edith Ham Stickle

Although the United States involvement was brief compared to that of Europe, World War I was a costly conflict, both for the country and for the state, in terms of lives lost and a disrupted economy. Within the state, the Red Cross was extremely active in raising money and preparing dressings and articles of clothing such as socks and gloves to send overseas. The end of the war ushered in a period of local and national prosperity and pride in the country, but the seeds had been sown for future events, and within little more than a decade the burgeoning wealth of the country was to take a sharp downturn, setting the stage for one of the more devastating periods in the history of the United States—that of the Great Depression.

Few people were prepared for the crash of the prosperous wave on which the country had been riding since the war. The situation was so desperate that for the first time in American history the government found it necessary to mobilize large-scale efforts to help people through relief programs.[29] In New York, as elsewhere in the country, extensive unemployment, hunger, and homelessness followed quickly on the heels of the stock market debacle that began in October 1929. However, Lorena Hickok, in a fact-finding tour of New York State for Harry L. Hopkins, the Federal Relief Administrator, reported, "...on a seven-day trip through the state...I found relief administration and adequacy so far ahead of what I had seen in other states that there just isn't any basis for comparison at all."[30]

The Great Depression created a "make-do" society. The old saying "Use it up/Wear it out/Make it do/Or do without" became the credo by which people had to live in order to survive. Women saved by patching clothes, reweaving socks, splitting sheets up the center and reseaming them edge to edge to equalize wear, cutting down adults' clothing for children, relining winter coats with old blankets, and storing trunks full of rags or anything else that might come in handy.[31] Many quilts were made as a result of this philosophy, and some of the lively scrap quilts registered by the Project from this period give credence to the old saw that "necessity is the mother of invention."

The Depression placed an additional burden on women, and many of the gains women had made in the period following World War I were abruptly wiped out, not to be recovered until World War II, when it became imperative for the nation to include women in the industrial work force. Worries about unemployment, where the next meal would come from, keeping a roof over your children's heads, or paying a doctor's bill could cause a debilitating depression, and apathy could quickly set in with enforced idleness. Some escape was needed, and contests became ideal popular pastimes during the Depression. They allowed the fantasy—as well as the

49. Fan Variation; made by Lillian Wells Ackerman Cooper (1880–1946); Schenectady, Schenectady County; 1920s–1930s; pieced and appliquéd cotton; 103″ x 84″. (Collection of Beatrice Sylvester) Lillian Wells Ackerman Cooper called this pattern Fan Variation, although it might more appropriately be termed a variation on the well-known Dresden Plate design. She used scraps from her children's clothes as well as bought yard goods in her quilts. Lillian Cooper received many of her quilt patterns from friends, and her daughter, the present owner of the quilt, has sketches of other quilts her mother made. The top of this one is pieced by machine but hand quilted by the daughter.

possibility—of winning and also helped to keep minds active. The 1933 Sears Roebuck Century of Progress quilt contest was one that captured women's imaginations, and almost 25,000 quilts were entered from all over the nation. One of those entries is shown here.

Those of the middle class who were lucky enough to have some income also had to learn how to make do and they did. Along with their poorer sisters, they learned how to ask unashamedly for feed and flour sacks to use for clothing or other sewing needs. And they would get together to quilt—the intellectual companionship and sociability provided by group activity could prove a balm for bruised spirits.[32] With the encouragement of the

The vast Sears family of customers and friends will have head-quarters of its own at Chicago's 1933 World's Fair, "A Century of Progress." A big, attractive, comfortable building where they can meet, rest, eat, write—in short, where they can feel perfectly "at home." You will be more than welcome.

The Fair will be open June 1 to November 1 and will outstrip in size and in interesting exhibits, its illustrious predecessor of '93, the World's Columbian Exposition.

In the very midst of the world's wonders, just inside one of the main gateways, we have built the beautiful structure pictured above, for your comfort and convenience.

Here you will find lounging quarters, rest rooms, check-room facilities, a complete information bureau to tell you about roads, railroads, and local transportation, and a telephone and telegraph office.

CENTURY OF PROGRESS
QUILTING CONTEST
$7,500 IN PRIZES

Do you quilt? If you do, you'll be interested in entering Sears great nationwide Quilting Contest, being held in connection with the Chicago World's Fair. Anyone may enter a quilt in this contest. At the close of the contest the winning quilts will be exhibited in the Sears building at the Fair.

For full particulars, write Sue Roberts, Home Advisor, for free circular 9452L. Address your letter to your nearest Sears mail order house.

The broad expanse of roof has been made into a delightful open deck overlooking a large portion of the grounds and swept by the refreshing breezes of Lake Michigan. There will be interesting exhibits of merchandise and manufacturing processes. They will be highly informative, you will enjoy them thoroughly, and you'll not be asked to buy!

The Sears building and the many free services it provides are yours while you're at the Fair. Use them; make this your headquarters; we want you to come and feel at ease.

If there is any special information you would like to have in advance of coming to the Fair, we will be glad to get it for you; and we will send you free on request a circular published by the Fair management, describing and picturing various buildings and other attractions. Please address your request to our nearest Mail Order House.

50. 1933 Century of Progress Exposition, Chicago, Illinois. (Courtesy Sears, Roebuck & Co.)

51. Transportation; made by Elizabeth Skelley Fitzgerald (1898–1985); Highland Falls, Orange County, 1933; pieced and appliquéd cotton; 82″ x 70″. (Collection of Margaret McDonald) This bright quilt was made for the Century of Progress quilt contest (which attracted almost 25,000 entries) sponsored by Sears, Roebuck & Co. in 1933, as part of the celebration of Chicago's hundredth anniversary. A letter dated June 15, 1933, written on behalf of the judges of the contest, informed the quiltmaker of who the winners were and stated that "more than 1700 quilts were received at our Philadelphia Mail Order House alone." The letter gave the criteria by which the prize-winning quilts were selected, thirty of which were displayed at the Sears Building in Chicago that summer. The prize money totaled $7,500.00, with the grand prize being $1,200—well worth competing for in the depth of the Great Depression.

The quiltmaker had researched each of the subjects, from covered wagon to motorcycle, to present them properly, and no two blocks are alike. She worked on the quilt many nights by candlelight until it was time for her to go to work as manager of a school cafeteria. In an interview in a local newspaper (*News of the Highlands*, July 17, 1975) when she was seventy-eight, she recalled that, "My grandmother taught me hemming and stitching on the muslin bags that staples such as sugar or flour came in. That's how I first learned quilting." Her daughter, the current owner, said that her mother was involved in quilting until her death and was one of the founders of the Quilters of the Hudson Highlands guild.

52. Ragged Robin; made by Hattie Teter (1878–1946); Livingstonville, Schoharie County; 1939; pieced cotton; 90″ x 75″. (Collection of Edith Kuhar) Hattie Teter, the grandmother of the owner, signed and dated this quilt in one of the corners. Hattie was a farm wife, and she helped the family finances by quilting tops brought to her and by selling some of her own quilts. She made quilts all winter long, and the family remembers that there were quilts on every bed in the house. She also made clothing for the family; some of the fabric in the quilt could have been from clothing scraps, but the owner recalls that in her childhood a large box filled with fabrics would arrive by mail for her grandmother, who would choose what she wanted and then send the balance back. This was the last quilt known to have been made by Hattie Teter.

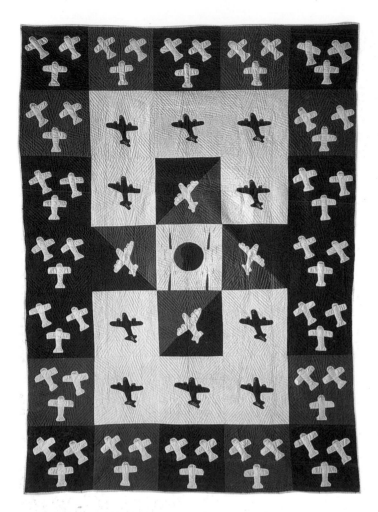

53. Airplane; made by Mrs. Baggs; Springfield Gardens, Queens County; 1939; pieced and appliquéd cotton; 101″ x 71″. (Collection of Brenda Fish) Charles A. Lindbergh's historic transoceanic flight in 1927 captured the imagination of the nation to an extraordinary degree and solidified the country's romance with flight. This fanciful appliquéd airplane design was undoubtedly made in honor of Lindbergh's flight, as were many other quilts with airplane motifs in that period. Mrs. Baggs was the friend of the present owner's mother-in-law.

churches, women banded together to make quilts for others; it was a charitable thing to do. What little extra money they had went into a fund to buy batting and they donated their old scraps or clothing for tops and backing.

The election of Franklin Delano Roosevelt in 1932 gave the country new hope for the future, and a gradual upswing in the economy—and living conditions—began to take place as domestic policy and adjusted aspirations took precedence over foreign policy. A temporary isolationism did not last, however, as, by 1938 and 1939, the recognition of impending war stimulated the revival of idle factories and put more people back to work. There is, perhaps, a certain irony in the fact that it took another war to bring about full recovery from the insidious effects of the Depression years.

Perhaps it was the World's Fair of 1939–1940 held in New York City, with its celebration of a century of achievements and its highlighting of current scientific marvels and prophecies of what was to come, that more

than anything else signaled the end of the dark era of the Depression to the populace and encouraged the vision of a "brave new world." The revitalization that had begun with Roosevelt and been fostered within the city and state by the incandescent Mayor Fiorello LaGuardia and capable Governor Herbert Lehman was working. Once more, New Yorkers were able to take pride in the "Empire State," in its far-reaching programs and growing quality of life. The unique and positive personality of each region of the state contributed much to its cultural, social, and economic well-being, the essence of which is reflected in the quilts and quiltmakers of the state.

This brings to a close an overview of the years covered by the New York Project in its documentation of quilts. New York has continued in the progressive mode that it set in its earliest days, and many events and activities have lent their further strength to the state over the intervening years. But that story—and the quilts that go with it—is for another time and another place.

55. Central Medallion; maker unknown; Haverstraw, Rockland County; c. 1825; cotton and chintz; 104″ x 100″. (Courtesy Laura Fisher/Antique Quilts & Americana, New York City) This unusually large quilt has a large variety of early printed fabrics in its borders. The plain area at the top was purposely left blank, for the bed pillows would rest here, making any design unnecessary. The central floral medallion with birds is done in Broderie Perse, an appliqué technique in which forms such as flowers, birds, foliage, and animals were cut out from larger pieces of printed of cotton and chintz and then stitched to a plain fabric. Stylistically, it derives from the Indian palampores so popular during the early part of the eighteenth century.

Images in Fabric
TECHNOLOGY, TRADE, AND TRANSMITTAL
OF TEXTILES IN NEW YORK STATE

New York's advantageous geographical location and its physical attributes were to make it a leader in both the manufacture and the trade of textiles, together with related commercial and industrial endeavors.

In theory, under neither Dutch nor British rule was manufacturing allowed in the colonies. There was a prohibition against the manufacture of textiles by the Dutch West India Company, the "owners" of New Netherland, but spinning and weaving were carried on from the early years of settlement. Once clothing and bedding items brought from the homeland were depleted and as supplies were expensive or in short supply, colonists turned their thoughts toward making their own, although importers continued to supply the majority of the needs until about 1750.[1]

The British Navigation Act of 1651 specified that goods from the colonies could be shipped only on British or colonial ships, and this was followed by further restrictions requiring merchandise imported to the colonies to be carried on English ships navigated by Englishmen.[2] Thus, whether imports or exports, all merchandise passed first through England, further increasing the cost to the final buyer. The restrictions encouraged home production as well as smuggling, and there were "reports from New York of 'everyone' making his own linen and a large part of his woolens" in order to bypass the restrictions and have affordable fabrics—or even any fabric at all.[3]

The 1699 Wool Act, which essentially forbade any wool exports from the colonies, was yet another measure intended to protect the British wool industry. A warning bell was sounded by Lord Cornbury, then governor of New York, in 1705 and was a portent of the events to come:

> ...want...sets men's wits to work, and that has put them upon a trade which, I am sure, will hurt England in a little time; for I am well informed that upon Long Island and Connecticut they are setting upon a woolen manufacture, and I myself have seen serge, made upon Long Island, that any man may

56. Whole Cloth; the maker, specific location, and date are unknown; calimanco; 96½" x 81". (Collection of Hinckley Museum, Ithaca, N.Y.) Very little is known about this beautiful quilt. It is made from glazed wool in sixteen-inch panels, and dyed a beautiful, vibrant red. Although the fabric, which is most likely homespun, cannot be precisely dated, it is thought to be from the late eighteenth or early nineteenth century, and the design and type of stitching are consistent with this period. The glazing was probably done by a professional; it was not unusual to find advertisements for such services in contemporary newspapers. One such notice, offering "Glazing executed in the first stile," appeared in the November 11, 1801 edition of *The New York Gazette and General Advertiser.*

57. Sampler; made by Mary-Ann Bennett (1851–1904); East Hampton, Suffolk County; late nineteenth century; pieced and appliquéd cotton; 90″ x 74″. (Collection of Olga Bennett Collins) The Bennett family, which has been engaged in farming and fishing on the eastern end of Long Island for many generations, refers to this as the "Wolf" quilt because Edward Bennett, an ancestor, earned bounties for killing four wolves, which are appliquéd on one of the blocks (see bottom row, third block from right). This colorful, eccentric, and intensely personal quilt consists of a top and bottom but no batt or binding; it has family history as well as some state history incorporated in its design. The quiltmaker, the owner's grandmother, included the initials of her children, and the appliquéd hand print is believed to be her own. The squirrel and acorn represent the oak trees in the area in which they lived, the horses and horseshoes the mode of travel, and the quail and other birds the local wild life. The Bennett ancestors migrated from England about 1639. The fourteenth generation of the family (the great-grandchildren of the quilt owner) remains in the area, although the family homestead and cemetery are now part of the Suffolk County Park and New York State Preservation Lands.

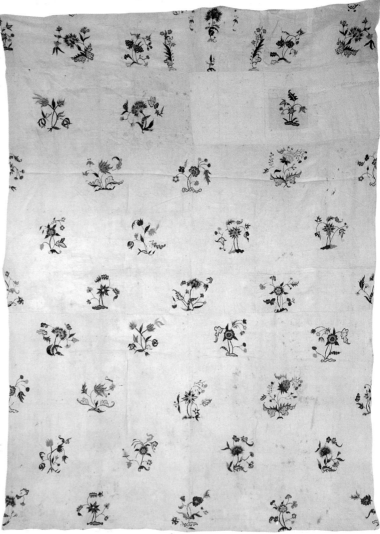

58. Whole Cloth with crewel embroidery; made by a member of the Osborne-Gould-Cook family; East Hampton, Suffolk County; late eighteenth century; unquilted linen with wool embroidery; 88″ x 86″. (Collection of Janet F. Lester) According to family history, this piece descended in the Osborne, Gould, and Cook families and was made in 1675, possibly by Martha Cooper Cook, daughter of John Cooper, an original settler who first brought his family to Massachusetts in 1635 and then in 1640 came to Southampton, Long Island. Martha, who was five in 1640, married another original settler, Ellis Cook. The family believed that the quilt was planned by Martha when she was about thirty-five or forty years old and made from wool sheared from the family's sheep and dyed with vegetable dyes from plants on the family's farm, and from linen made from the flax grown by the family. After an examination based on design and execution and comparison with comparable pieces at the Fashion Institute of Technology in New York, it was decided that the work was more likely to have been made toward the end of the eighteenth century, so Martha could not have been its maker.

wear. Now, if they begin to make serge, they will, in time, make coarse cloth and then fine.... I hope I may be pardoned if I declare my opinion to be that all these Colloneys, which are but twigs belonging to the main tree—England—ought to be kept entirely dependent upon and subservient to England, and that can never be if they are suffered to go on in the notions they have that, as they are Englishmen, soe they may set up their same manufactures here as people may do in England; for the consequence will be, if once they can see they can cloathe themselves,... without the help of England, they, who are not very fond of submitting to government, would soon think of putting in execution designs they had long harboured in their breasts. This will not seem strange, when you consider what sort of people this country is inhabited by.[4]

In spite of Lord Cornbury's warning, home production flourished and continued to be an important unit of production for the colonists. Flax was the major early fiber; it was easily grown in New York's temperate climate and the necessary water resources were available for retting to produce linen cloth. A type of native flax was grown by American Indians and used extensively for nets and cord, but more refined varieties were also brought in by the European settlers.[5]

The cold New York winters made wool a necessary and important fiber for cloth, as Lord Cornbury had noted. Sheep raising was encouraged by the community, and early town records note regulations with respect to sheep breeding, to "common watering places," and to the fencing of sheep to insure protection against wolves.[6] That wolves were an early menace has been well documented in local histories.[7] A 1643 Southampton town record states that ten shillings would be paid for the head of every wolf brought to the magistrate, and in 1663 East Hampton granted the right to build wolf pits in order to save livestock. Hempstead records show that one Thomas Landon received six pounds as bounty for killing six wolves, and a 1683 statute stated that, "whatsoever Christian shall kill a grown wolf on Long Island he shall be paid twenty shillings." Indians were also eligible for bounties, but they did not earn as much.[8] Bounties, sometimes amounting to as much as $50 a head, continued to be offered as settlement spread west in the early years of the nineteenth century, and hunts had been so successful by the mid-century mark that wolves have yet to reappear in the state.[9] One quilt documented during the course of the Project celebrates an ancestor's success in claiming wolf bounties.

Abundant and varied vegetation yielded sources for natural dyes for both wool and linen, and some of the earliest quilts documented show their evidence. By 1696 on Long Island, local carding and fulling mills were dressing and dyeing cloth produced in the home. In areas where fulling mills were not yet available, neighbors

59. Double Irish Chain; descended in the Porter and Chapman families; New York City; early nineteenth century; pieced cotton; 106″ x 102″. (Collection of Mrs. John B. Turner, Jr.) According to the present owner, this quilt has always been in the family although the quiltmaker is unknown. It is one of the earliest Irish Chain patterns seen during the Project, and some of the fabrics may actually be late eighteenth century and possibly of European or English origin. A replica of this quilt was also registered and is said to have been made by the daughter of the maker of this one.

might gather together and hold a "fulling bee"—an event where chairs were placed in a circle and participants sat and stamped the wet, soaped fabric on the floor with their bare feet in order to finish it.

The country saw a surge in textile imports following the end of the French and Indian War, but a 1764 Act passed to help England pay its war debts again placed heavy taxes on textile imports in the colonies. The repressive legislation not only continued to push the colonies toward independence but also led to a growing capacity for home manufacture and small-scale textile production that served the country well when it finally went to war with the mother country. The Revolutionary War did not, however, bring textile imports to a halt; in fact, there is some indication that New York City at times received almost its regular supply of textiles between what was brought in directly from other countries or from privateering sorties.[10]

At the conclusion of the Revolutionary War there was an initial drop in home and local production and a rise in imports until it was recognized that such production was

60. Georgetown Circle; maker unknown; possibly Salt Point, Dutchess County; c. 1850; pieced cotton; 100¾″ x 81″. (Collection of Alfred Hasbrouck) This quilt was found in the house where the owner's mother was born, but no other information about it is available. The house is in Salt Point, Dutchess County. The fabrics that make up the circles—particularly the brown and blue prints—are early, but the sashing may be mid-century or somewhat later.

crucial for the fledgling nation as a means of maintaining industrial as well as political independence. This brought about a concerted effort to improve both the size and capabilities of textile manufacture in this country as well as the quality of the materials produced.

In December 1789, the New York Manufacturing Society had in its employ fourteen weavers and over 130 spinners, and one of them was Samuel Slater, an Englishman who had served an apprenticeship under Jedediah Strutt, the partner of Richard Arkwright, the inventor of the water frame for spinning. Slater eventually took his skills to Rhode Island, where he built Arkwright machines from memory and began the revolutionizing of American manufacture.

By 1800, although woolen cloth was still being produced in the home, small carding mills began to be found in almost every township in New York state where water power was available.[11] Shortly thereafter the first cotton mills were incorporated in Oneida County, with technology brought by New Englanders moving west in search of better farm lands. By 1810 there were twenty-six cotton mills in the state.[12]

A combination of factory and domestic manufacture continued in rural areas of the state throughout the first quarter of the nineteenth century, especially in the western part where access to stores was minimal or required long trips. In 1822 one family in that area produced "319 yards of linen cloth, 25 of kersey for bags, 32 of shirting, 35 of diaper, 54 of cotton and linen, 199 of woolen cloth, 16 of kersey for blankets, 24 of plain flannel for blankets, 28 of cotton and wool, 34 of cotton, 22 of worsted...5 bed quilts, 1 carpet...1 bed tick, 7 blankets, 10 flannel sheets, 20 linen sheets...and 12 kersey bags," as well as 147 items of clothing, from socks to coats—and this in addition to all the usual farm and household tasks![13]

The cotton industry spread west along the Mohawk Valley from the Hudson, and, by the time the Erie Canal opened in 1825, many cities and towns in the western part

61. Starburst variation; made by Jane Smith Phillips Wells (1794–1874); Peconic, Suffolk County; mid nineteenth century; pieced cotton chintz; 91″ x 90″. (Collection of Katharine Mayne) This masterful quilt presents an encyclopedic array of the print fabrics of the time in a favorite design. The quiltmaker, Jane Smith Phillips, married Giles Wells and lived her entire life in the village of Peconic. She is the great-great-great-grandmother of the present owner.

62. Jane Smith Phillips Wells

45

of the state had some type of textile industry. Fulling, carding, shearing, dyeing, and bleaching had now all become specialized trades, and much of the technical know-how for operation and repair of textile machinery was supplied by British immigrants until well into the century.

The War of 1812 again reduced imports and, with American nationalism at a fever pitch, the textile industry gained a permanent foothold. Legislation quickened the process by creating high tariffs on imports and exempting textile mills from taxation and textile workers from jury and military service. As factory textile manufacture became more widespread and fabrics became cheaper, household manufacture correspondingly dropped. Between 1825 and 1835 it decreased by nearly fifty percent, although one source notes that as late as 1835 over 230,000 yards of fabric—mostly woolens and linens—were produced by "housewives and professional weavers in back rooms and attics."[14]

By 1840 the production of textiles occupied a preeminent rank in the manufacturing industry of the state. In that year, New York listed 323 woolen mills, with 4,636 employees and a product value of over three and a half million dollars,[15] and by the time of the Civil War as many as thirty cotton and other textile mills existed in Rensselaer County alone.[16]

By 1850, the port of New York was still importing and distributing foreign fabrics equal in amount to the total American textile manufacture—about sixty million dollars' worth.[17] The city had early on been selected by the British as the place to dump surplus textiles, and ambitious entrepreneurs had capitalized by creating textile auctions. These auctions brought in thousands of merchants and shopkeepers looking for bargains that they could then resell at a nice profit to textile-hungry dwellers in rural areas.

The geographical location of New York City favored its establishment as the center of the country's textile trade, as was well being recognized by contemporary chroniclers:

This city is esteemed the most eligible situation for commerce in the United States; it almost necessarily commands the trade of one-half of New Jersey, most of that of Connecticut, and part of that of Massachusetts, besides the whole fertile interior country, which is penetrated by one of the largest rivers in America. This city imports most of the goods consumed between a line of thirty miles east of the Connecticut River, and twenty miles west of the Hudson, which is 130 miles; and between the ocean and the confines of Canada, about 250 miles: a considerable portion of which is the best populated of any part of the United States.... In times of peace, New York will command more commercial business than any town in the United States.[18]

The Hudson River opened up the interior of the state to the transport of textiles and other goods. Later, with the construction of the Erie Canal, the New York businessman was able to reach the very outposts of the western frontier.

New York's natural harbor also promoted coastal trading, which led in turn to Manhattan merchants gaining control of the large export trade of cotton. A "cotton triangle" was created, with cotton ports in the south shipping directly to Liverpool and LeHavre and having their ships return via New York with immigrants and cloth manufactured abroad. There the ships would take on new cargoes and sail for their southern home ports. Many times only two sides of the triangle would be used—the southern ports would ship their goods directly to New York, thus permitting New York to export cotton to European ports, while foreign finished textiles would be sent to New York for redistribution to the rest of the country.[19]

By the time of the Civil War, Americans were buying most of their fabrics through New York firms. Imports remained the outstanding feature of New York's seaport business, and the merchant houses of Manhattan had a virtual monopoly on woolen and cotton goods from England, linens from Ireland, and silks and laces from France. Worth Street in lower Manhattan became the international center for fabrics, and the city has continued into this century as a major force in the textile trade. Textile manufacturing in the state began to decrease

63. Small fabric mills in the Mohawk River Valley and other parts of the state were an important component of the New York State economy into the opening years of the twentieth century. (Courtesy John Jackson Glass Negative Collection)

46

64. Central Medallion; made by Louisa Wells Fitz (1845–1908); Southold, Suffolk County; date unknown; pieced and appliquéd cotton; 35″ x 32½″. (Collection of James Henry Rich, Jr.) This unusual crib quilt was made by Louisa Wells Fitz, who was the daughter of Henry Fitz (1810–1863), a telescope maker. A wax model of her father grinding a telescope lens and a telescope that he made for Vassar College are now in the collection of the Smithsonian Institution. Louisa lived in the town of Southold on the north fork of eastern Long Island, and married Silas Overton. The fabrics and style of the work would indicate an earlier date for the quilt than the maker's age suggests, but her signature on the back and family history denotes Louisa as the maker. The family notes that she was still single at the time it was made, but there is no information about why it was made. It is now owned by the great-grandson of the maker.

65. Delectable Mountains; made by Aurelia Loomis Root (1820–1903); Buffalo, Erie County; c. 1840; pieced cotton; 92″ x 94″. (Collection of Mrs. Howard N. Knowles) Aurelia Loomis was born in Warren, New York, a seventh-generation American. On January 10, 1837, at the age of seventeen, she married Birdsey A. Root. They spent the first ten years of their married life in Albany, and sometime between 1850 and 1860 they moved to Buffalo, where Birdsey was employed by the Western Transportation Company, Erie Basin-Buffalo. It appears that the Roots were people of some means and that Aurelia had a certain amount of financial independence—which was rather unusual for women in the nineteenth century—as she is known to have purchased a $500 Civil War bond in 1861 in her own right. She also established a reputation for being active in charitable causes. The blue fabrics, typical of the period, are printed with designs of flowers, ferns, and fruit. The quilt is now owned by Aurelia's great-granddaughter.

66. Aurelia Loomis Root

67. Star of Bethlehem/Rising Sun; made by Mary (Betsy) Totten (1781–1861); Tottenville, Staten Island; 1825–1835; pieced and appliquéd cotton; 94¼″ x 96⅛″. (Collection of Smithsonian Institution, Washington, D.C.; Gift of Mrs. Marvel Mildred Matthes) This spectacularly ornate Star of Bethlehem—called Rising Sun by the quiltmaker, Mary (Betsy) Totten—contains eleven different roller-printed cottons, of which only four have one color added by surface roller. There are some discharge prints, and the green fabric is a true one-step green; it has not been overprinted. The quilt has the initials "BT" cross-stitched in rose silk at the foot of the vase in one corner. Mary Totten was one of seven children born to Gilbert Totten and Mary Butler in 1781. She was twice married, first to the Reverend Joseph Polhemus and then to Matthew Williams. She died in 1861, leaving no children. She is known to have made several quilts, which are now in various museum collections: the Smithsonian, the Staten Island Historical Society (Richmondtown Restoration), and the New York State Historical Association in Cooperstown.

significantly from the latter part of the nineteenth century, however, and by the 1920s few of the earlier mills or print works were still in operation; the base of production had changed to the southern states.

New York, as a leader in the textile industry, also produced the first and foremost textile designer of the nineteenth century, Candace Wheeler (1827–1923), who was born in Delhi, New York. In 1877, Wheeler organized the New York Society of Decorative Art, which encouraged women of artistic talent to produce marketable works, and in 1878, she helped found the New York Women's Exchange, where women could sell well-made wares. In later years, Associated American Artists, which had originally included Louis C. Tiffany and others as well as Wheeler, began to produce fabrics for the home that were both experimental and wonderful studies in color, and many mill owners adopted their designs and color schemes. Ultimately, her designs were to be found on inexpensive printed cottons, chintzes, and denims as well as the more luxurious silks, velvets, and brocades, for she wanted women of all economic levels to have access to good design.

Wheeler's work promoted the employment of American women in textile work, and she had a far-reaching influence on home decoration. Her influence in the quilting of the times may be seen in many Crazy quilts, both in embroidery and appliqué patterns as well as in the naturalistic forms that she took directly from nature.[20]

Although some eighteenth-century advertisements for local fabric printers exist, in general, textile printing was not a well-developed technique in this country until the nineteenth century, and most people depended on the trade with Europe and the East for their printed fabrics. Prints were always popular and coveted, and it is probable that some block printing of linen was carried on at home or on a small-scale commercial basis in this country from fairly early on.[21] Indian palampores and Indian and European chintzes were always desirable, and some quilts were located that showed use of these fabrics in their construction. In the late eighteenth century, John Hewson of Philadelphia made his name famous with his superb and colorful block prints, and although some contemporary printing shops in New York are known from newspaper advertisements, none whose work is comparable to Hewson's have been identified.

There is one type of fabric that seems to have been peculiar to eastern New York State and—some say—to the Connecticut River Valley, although there is no clear agreement on the origin, production location, or even the method of production of these prints.[22] These so-called "blue-resist prints" date from the eighteenth century and have large floral or leaf designs in indigo blue on white grounds. They seem to have been done in a reverse method to the typical resist pattern that came out of India, but no good documentation on them has yet been found.

68. Quilted counterpane; maker unknown; New York City; mid nineteenth century; cotton; 89⅜″ x 72⅞″. (Collection of Smithsonian Institution, Washington, D.C.) Much of the fabric in this quilt dates from the late eighteenth century even though the quilt is believed to have been made quite a bit later. Both front and back are made of pieces of cotton plate-printed with pastoral and classical motifs that include two boys riding leopards. The cloth was printed at the Bromley Hall Printworks, considered one of the most important of the early printworks in England, in 1785 and sold under the name "Tyger," even though the jungle cat bears more resemblance to a leopard than a tiger. It is thought that the fabric had been used before, possibly for bed hangings. The block-printed border was probably the trim used on the original bed curtains. The quilt is said to have been owned by William Paulding, mayor of New York 1823–1828, most probably after he left office and took up residence at Lyndhurst, his palatial home built in 1838 in Tarrytown, New York.

Some quilts were seen that contained these fabrics, but it proved to be impossible to locate them firmly within New York State and so they are not included here.

Discharge printing was a popular method of the early nineteenth century and gives somewhat the same appearance as a resist print. Discharge printing, however, removes color from color after dyeing, rather than protecting the fabric from the dye as in resist work.[23] The

69. Bars and Diamonds; maker unknown; Glens Falls, Warren County; c. 1830; linen toile, cotton; 96″ x 96″. (Collection of Susan Parrish Antiques, New York City) Two toiles, one blue-printed and one red-printed, are joined with a darker cotton chintz to form a dramatically simple quilt. The toiles are of the toile de Jouy type and are probably somewhat earlier than the other fabrics used in the quilt.

process may be combined with other methods to provide prints with multiple colors, and several of the earlier quilts seen had excellent examples of discharge prints in their piecing or appliqué work.

Block printing was used both here and abroad until well into the nineteenth century, but by the late eighteenth century copperplate printing was becoming a popular method. Copperplate prints were frequently large floral repeats or complex scenes of everything from battles to everyday life. These prints were generally monochromatic, in blues, browns, greens, or maroons, the most famous of which were the highly coveted "toile de Jouy" (literally, "fabrics from Jouy"), a fine linen printed fabric. The early prints from Christophe Oberkampf's famous print works in Jouy, France, were first done from hand-cut wooden blocks and were usually small florals in monochromatic or several colors; when Oberkampf switched to copperplate printing, however, the character of the prints changed dramatically, and they became story-telling fabrics from which we are still learning today. By 1800, Oberkampf had begun to use metal-roller technology, which was rapidly changing the English printing industry, although it did not reach the United States for several more years, and it is about then that the term *toile* began to be used for any type of heroic or pastoral scenic print on linen, regardless of its source.[24] Several outstanding quilts containing copperplate prints—one almost certainly containing a toile de Jouy—were located during the Project.

The first successful roller prints began to be made in Europe in the latter part of the eighteenth century, but proper registration remained a problem well into the nineteenth century, although the great variety of designs that roller printing made available made up in some respects for the lack of quality. Sometimes hand-block printers were employed to finish coloring roller-printed cloths to improve the quality, and it is often difficult to distinguish between the prints produced only by wooden surface rollers or by hand blocks used in conjunction with engraved rollers.

Roller printing began to be used in the United States about 1810 and was well established by 1825, mostly at factories and mills in New England. One of the major print works in New York was the Hudson Calico Print Works at Stockport, founded in 1826 by Joseph and Benjamin Marshall, brothers who had emigrated from Scotland earlier in the century. By 1836 it had forty-two hand-block printers, two four-color printing machines, and three that printed in three colors. The machines had been imported from England, and each could produce in one day an amount of printed cloth equal to that of the forty-two hand-block printers.[25] A number of quilts were registered that include what appear to be roller-printed fabrics; whether they are of New York—or even American—manufacture is open to question. However, very few American printed textiles of this period can be firmly documented, and the close relationship between the British and American industries have led to many similarities in pattern.[26]

Roller printing encouraged a certain amount of experimentation and innovation in design, and the so-called rainbow prints—done via a technique that used graduated shades of one or more colors to create a rainbow-like effect—that grew out of this caught the popular imagination and were used extensively in clothing and quilts. The more skillful and careful of the quiltmakers who used these prints could position them to give a sense of texture and depth. Rainbow shading is said to have been used in block printing as early as the 1820s, but roller presses made it a far more common technique after about 1840.[27]

By the 1860s and 1870s roller printing was being used to create the seemingly endless variety of colorful—and cheap—cotton calico prints that became a staple fabric for clothing and quilts. The twentieth century saw the stabilization of printed fabrics in many forms, but less and

70. Sunburst; made by Sarah Emily Wells Tuthill (1834–1913); eastern Long Island; c. 1860; pieced cotton; 82″ x 70″. (Collection of Thomas C. and Mary K. Ryan) Sarah Emily Wells Tuthill was the daughter of Daniel and Eveline Wells. She and her husband, Charles Henry Tuthill, had one son, Clarence, who was born in 1859 and died in 1928, leaving no children. The quilt she left as part of her legacy is made of very fine fabrics, primarily roller-printed chintzes, and the techniques used show that she was a skilled needlewoman. Both this quilt and a Crazy quilt also attributed to her and seen at a Quilt Day on eastern Long Island were purchased from antiques dealers by the present owners, and the information known about the quilts was supplied by the dealers.

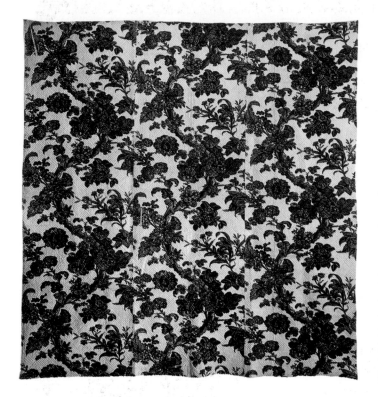

71. Whole Cloth; made by Prudence Pierson Halsey (1765–1851); Sagaponack, Suffolk County; late eighteenth–early nineteenth century; roller-printed cotton; 96" x 88". (Collection of Janet F. Lester) This whole-cloth quilt was made by the great-great-great-grandmother of the present owner. Prudence Pierson married William Halsey, a farmer of Bridgehampton, Long Island, on June 7, 1787. The family story is that this quilt was made from bed curtains. The quilt top is made of three thirty-inch panels roller-printed in a naturalistic design, with a panel repeat of thirty-five inches. There are two places in the print where the ink missed the textile; it is possible that the fabric wrinkled while going under the printing plate, thus leaving a narrow white streak in the design.

less printing was done in New York. By 1930, *The Blue Book Textile Directory of the United States and Canada* no longer has any listings for New York; by the 1940s, most print work had been transferred to the South, although some was still being done in New England.[28]

The earliest settlers had a limited number of fabrics available to them—especially when they had to rely on those produced at home or otherwise locally—but by the end of the seventeenth century a wide range of imported silks, linens, woolens, and cottons could be had, as long as the buyer could pay the price. As the state became more settled and fabric production began in earnest, a greater variety of locally produced cottons, linens, and woolens began to be more widely available. Although there was a great enthusiasm for silk production in the first half of the nineteenth century (in 1845, some production in twenty-nine counties was reported[29]), attempts were largely unsuccessful, and only the Oneida Community had a silk industry of any size. Thus, silk fabrics remained largely imports until the latter part of the nineteenth century, when other states developed a more viable silk industry.

Calimanco, a wool satin that was often heavily glazed and frequently dyed in bright and lively colors, was the fabric of choice for bed furnishings in early colonial times. The New York Quilt Project located a number of whole-cloth quilts made of this fabric, many of them dating from the latter part of the eighteenth century. One example, part of the collection of the Buffalo-Erie Historical Society, is dyed with walnut hulls, and another of similar

coloration and style, although less elaborately stitched, was found in the New York State Museum collection. The quilting on such pieces tends to be exquisite, as the simple fabric, with its polished surface, serves as a perfect background to show off the skills of the maker. Although some of the calimanco fabric may have been made within the state, it is virtually impossible to tell whether the fabrics were foreign or locally made, as the technology of the time was not highly developed and essentially identical on both sides of the Atlantic.

Almost every type of fabric known to have been available in New York State has appeared in one or another of the quilts registered during the course of the Project. In some cases, selectively used and carefully placed prints hint at a scarcity of a certain fabric, or its importance to the maker. Some quilts were clearly "scrap-bag" creations (with many women believing in the concept of "waste not, want not"), while the structure of other quilts indicates that fabrics were purchased specifically for the design.

Once production had moved out of the home, women bought their fabrics in local general stores or relied on occasional trips to larger business centers where they could stock up on necessary items. General stores were ubiquitous (the 1845 state census listed over 12,000 retail stores); they were the first "department stores" and even those in the smallest towns offered their patrons a wide range of goods. The owners of these stores got their merchandise during semi-annual purchasing trips to New

72 and 72a. Feathered Star variation; made by Ellen McKnight Brayton (1807–1877); Westernville, Oneida County; c. 1840; pieced cotton and chintz with stuffed work; 102″ x 102″. (Collection of Katherine F. Sterling) Ellen McKnight Brayton married Milton Brayton of Westernville in May 1830 in Reading, Pennsylvania, where she was born and raised. Milton Brayton's father, George Brayton, was a founding father and the town clerk of Westernville in 1797 and also operated the first store in the area. Ellen and Milton settled permanently in Westernville in 1834, when their first child was born. According to Jeannette Lasansky of the Oral Traditions Project in Pennsylvania, there is a similarity in design to certain Pennsylvania quilts that seem to be clustered in the Cumberland/Dauphin counties area; this would suggest that Ellen might have seen the design earlier but created her own unique adaptation. The fabric used is typical of the imported roller-printed furnishing fabrics of the 1830s–1840s. It appears that the fabric was specifically purchased for this quilt, and it is obvious that the quilt had been rarely used, if at all (the staining is a result of water damage that occurred during the quilt's storage). The chintz still has its original glaze and the pencil markings for the quilting designs are still visible. The stuffed work in this quilt is extraordinarily fine.

72a. Detail

73. London Square; maker unknown; Skaneateles, Cayuga County; 1840–1862; pieced cotton; 97″ x 78″. (Collection of Margaret Evans Bennett) This quilt was the only London Square pattern seen during the entire registration process for the Project. The rainbow fabric was most likely bought specifically for this quilt, as the amount of material required for the pattern is far more than would normally have been left over from another project. The present owner received this quilt as a wedding gift from a family friend.

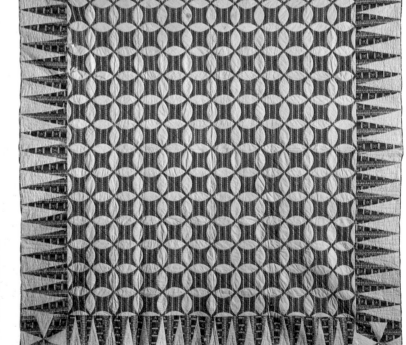

74. Orange Peel; maker unknown; Bedford, Cross River, Westchester County; mid nineteenth century; pieced cotton; 92″ x 83″. (Collection of George McTavey) The quiltmaker was a great-grandmother of the present owner, whose family had a farm in the Cross River section of Bedford. The quilt contains some fine early fabrics, including a popular blue-and-brown print.

75. Trip Around the World; made by Mary Janette Thompson Rifenback (1847–1914); Sidney Center, Delaware County; c. 1860; pieced cotton; 87″ x 74″. (Collection of Jane E. Higgins-Caranci) Mary Janette Thompson was the wife of a farmer, Stephen George Rifenback. The quilt is one of two that she made in the same pattern but in different colors. The present owner is a great-granddaughter of the quiltmaker.

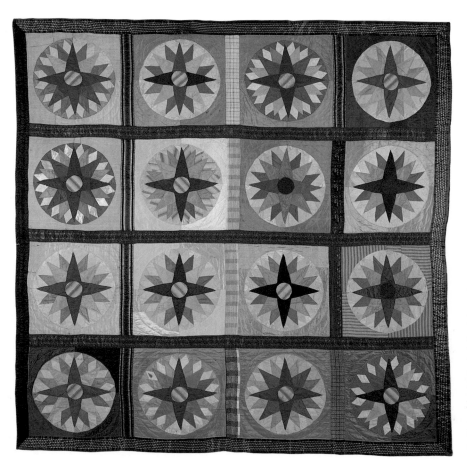

76. Mariner's Compass; made by Sarah Seymour Decker; Dunkirk, Chautauqua County; c. 1880; pieced silk and cotton; 91″ x 90¼″. Photograph by Mark Gulezian. (Collection of DAR Museum, Washington, D.C.; Gift of Doris Clark) This is the only example seen during the Project of a Mariner's Compass pattern (also known as Blazing Star, Compass Star, or Rising Sun, among other names) being executed in silk. Most examples were made of cotton, which seemed to be the preferred fabric, probably because the many points required by the design were less difficult to handle in the lighter fabric. It is interesting to compare other examples of Mariner's Compass quilts included in this book (see pages ii, 7, and 14) with this quilt; as a general rule, those made of cotton have a greater number of points as well as more slender points and finer stitching than those made of wool or silk.

77. Log Cabin—original design; made by Henriette Maria Frederike Caroline Schroeder Segcbarth (1860–1925); Dunkirk, Chautauqua County; 1890–1900; pieced silk and velvet; 89″ x 77½″. (Collection of John W. Segebarth) Henriette Maria Frederike Caroline Schroeder was born in the province of Pomerania, Prussia, and was brought to this country at the age of one in 1861. Her family settled in Dunkirk in Chautauqua County, and there she married William C. Segebarth, a custom tailor, in 1875. The quilt was made from lining scraps from her husband's tailoring business, and the chevron border is a particularly original touch. The current owner is a grandson and there are nine great-grandchildren living.

78. Whole Cloth; made by Katharine Killey Walbridge (1766–1848); Quaker Hill, Dutchess County; c.1798; cotton and wool; 96″ x 92½″. (Collection of New York State Museum, Albany, N.Y.) Very little information is known about this quilt other than the maker's name and birth and death dates. Like others of its type, the plain glazed ground serves as a background show-case for the exquisite stitching. A whole-cloth quilt owned by the Buf-falo-Erie Historical Society of similar style and color is said to have been dyed with walnut hulls.

79. Four Patch variation; made by Jennie Hess; probably Albany County; c. 1900; pieced cotton; 91″ x 78″. (Collection of Lydia VonLinden) Simple One Patch piecing forms the background for shimmering bars of miniature Four Patch blocks set on the diagonal. The maker, Jennie Hess of Preston Hollow, Albany County, was a friend of the owner's family; no one knows why this quilt was given to the family, but it has provided both visual and tactile delight through the years. Lydia VonLinden, the present owner, was born in 1903 and is the daughter of the quiltmaker Hattie Teter (see page 37).

80. The general storekeeper waits for customers to appear and finger the bolts of cloth on display at the dry-goods counter. (Courtesy John Jackson Glass Negative Collection)

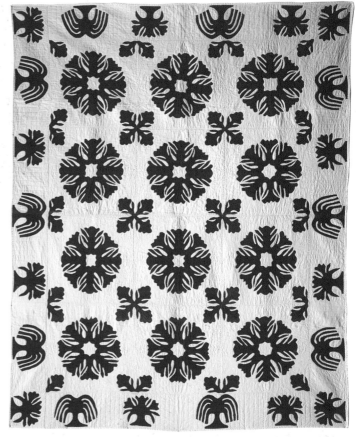

81. Snowflake with Tree border; made by Elsie Arnold Ives (1813–1882); New York; c. 1850; cotton; 90″ x 72″. (Collection of Barbara Hunt) There is no personal information about the quiltmaker known by her present descendants other than the fact that she made several quilts, most of them pieced, which are now in the possession of members of the family. The present owner of this quilt is the great-great-granddaughter-in-law of the maker; she notes that the quilt top was given to her by her mother-in-law, who had it quilted by a local quiltmaker about eight years ago. An examination revealed repairs to the top and a later backing. This quilt, like others seen from this area, has an interior design based on repetitive cut-outs and a border composed of two types of "weeping" trees. The tree border seems to have been a particularly popular motif of the region and the period.

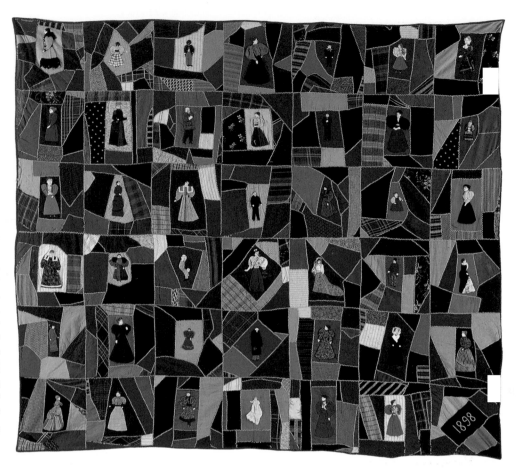

82. Crazy; made by Leila Butts Utter; Otsego County; 1898; pieced and appliquéd wool and cotton; 84" x 76". (Courtesy America Hurrah Antiques, New York City) Forty-one fashion plates of the 1860s through the 1890s—male and female, old and young—adorn this unique Crazy quilt. Both costumes and coiffures are painstakingly detailed, and facial features are delicately rendered with strands of thread. Leila Butts was an adopted child. She married James Utter, owner of a 168-acre farm, and they became foster parents to Elizabeth Munson, whom they regarded as their daughter, when she was two. In 1883, the name of James Utter appears as a subscriber to a fund for the Methodist Church in nearby Davenport (Delaware County), and it was likely that Leila was also a member of that church. This very special quilt has been extensively documented in Sandi Fox's book, *Wrapped in Glory*.

83. Trip Around the World; made by Ethel Roney's grandmother; Green County; 1885; pieced cotton; 94" x 78". (Collection of Kellee Esposito) This Trip Around the World has the date 1885 embroidered in outline stitch on the back. The quilt was given to the current owner by her grandmother as a wedding gift; however, there is no blood tie to the quiltmaker, who was identified only as "Ethel Roney's grandmother," from Greene County. (Ethel Roney, a close friend of the present owner's grandmother, died at the age of ninety-two in 1981.) The careful use of fabric suggests that fabric was purchased specifically for this quilt; one row is particularly intriguing because a tiger's face has been carefully cut from the fabric to show in each block.

84. Turkey in the Tree; maker and date unknown; Rockland County; cotton; 107″ x 92″. (Collection of Judith and Patrick Lawlor) This bright and lively silhouette quilt was purchased at an auction, where the auctioneers told the present owners that it had come from the home of a family descended from Alexander Hamilton, who had a home in the Ramapo Mountains of Rockland County. This is a summer quilt without a batt, and the pattern and the choice of Turkey Red fabric mean that it was probably made after 1850.

York City or by placing orders by mail or with traveling salesmen. The goods were then shipped throughout the state via the Erie Canal and railroads. The typical general store before the Civil War would have stocked about 250 different kinds of items, including from 3,000 to 4,000 yards of bolted cloth of different kinds and numerous sewing implements and accessories.[30] Thimbles, those most necessary of sewing implements, were manufactured throughout most of the nineteenth century by the silversmiths of Huntington, Long Island, among whom the best-known was Ezra C. Prime. By 1860, Prime and members of his family were not only the largest manufacturers of thimbles for the entire nation but were also exporting their wares.

Although we tend to think of the quiltmakers as the immediate and primary purchasers of fabric, in many cases this may not have been so, particularly if a woman lived in a place where there were few outlets for purchase. In 1853, for example, Emily and Abiathar Watkins re-

ceived a letter from Emily's sister Mary requesting "3/8 of a yard of muslin edging this width [width drawn] not very expensive but nice and send by Abiathar, and I will pay him; you can write the price."[31] Frequently, it was the husband or father who made the trips to town or to the larger commercial centers, and, although their women-folk may have charged them with specific requests in regard to types and colors of fabric, often the men would be faced with choices that did not necessarily match the requests and so made their own substitutions to meet the needs (or, perhaps, even their tastes!).

For many years, peddlers in rural areas, traveling on foot, horse, or by wagon, carried on an itinerant trade in various household items, including those needed for sewing, such as thimbles, needles, thread, and even yard goods. If a specific item was unavailable, the peddler might take an order and supply the requested item on his next circuit. In the case of fabrics, the peddler might also serve as the final arbiter of color and pattern if the specific piece were not available at his supply depot. Peddlers also served as a source for quilt designs; they might pass on information about patterns or templates for a popular pattern, or, in some cases, they might even provide an original pattern in exchange for a night's lodging or a meal; these latter, usually done as free-hand papercut templates bearing a remarkable resemblance to the "scherenschnitte," the highly decorative "scissors cutting" of paper of the Pennsylvania Germans, might explain some of the unusual and one-of-a-kind patterns that have shown up among the nineteenth-century quilts registered. By about 1870, the itinerant peddler was rapidly disappearing, but in the more rural parts of the state the peddler continued right up to the era of the automobile.

The fabrics seen in the quilts reviewed for the Project also reflected the prevailing tastes and fads of the times in which the quilts were made and showed that quilts served as fashionable reflections of their times. Patterns waxed and waned in popularity, as did the use of certain fabrics—although availability undoubtedly played a part in the latter. Identical prints or particular colors appeared time after time in quilts from far-flung reaches of the state, reflecting both availability and popularity.

Calicos were outstandingly popular in the early to mid nineteenth century. Everybody wanted them, and they were used extensively in both pieced and appliquéd quilts. By 1858, however, they were beginning to be disdained in the popular writings of the times: "Of the patchwork with calico I have nothing to say. Valueless indeed must be the time of that person who can find no better use for it than to make ugly counterpanes and quilts of pieces of cotton," lamented one such writer.[32] At the same time, as silks and velvets became more common and available on a broader scale, their use for quilts began to be extolled, and any woman with some leisure time and reasonable wealth was likely to want to try her skills with

85. Star of Bethlehem; maker unknown; possibly Sullivan County; late nineteenth century; pieced silk; 96″ x 96″. (Collection of Museum of American Folk Art, New York City; purchase made possible with funds from The Great American Quilt Festival II, 1990.15.1) This stunning quilt descended in the family of Jeremiah Sullivan Black, a famous lawyer who was Attorney General of the United States in 1857 under President James Buchanan. Although a native of Pennsylvania, he and his family lived in Sullivan County, New York, for a period. His daughter Mary, a physician, was also married to a physician, Lemuel R. Hurlbut, and they both practiced in Lockport, New York, for many years. This quilt was left to Marie Smith, their office nurse and good friend. At her death, the quilt was passed on to her daughter, Mary S. Lehmann, who offered it to the Museum about a year after it was seen during the Quilt Days.

these fabrics. Regardless of this trend that continued through the end of the nineteenth century, the use of calico survived; whether this is a tribute to the independent minds of the quiltmakers or an ongoing response to the utilitarian rather than the purely decorative—and especially the need to provide warmth at a reasonable price—is hard to say!

Technology and fashion dictated the color contents of quilts as well.[33] Prior to the discovery of aniline dyes in 1856 the reliance on natural dyes made for a somewhat limited color palette and one that could not always be counted on to produce colors of identical value and hue. By 1869, when synthetic dyes were truly competitive with natural ones, this problem was largely eliminated and certain colors—such as Fast Red A (better known as Turkey Red) in the late 1870s and 1880s and an artificial indigo in the 1890s—gained an overwhelming popularity and were seen with great frequency in quilts. Both these colors were favorites for fundraiser quilts, perhaps because of their easy availability, their colorfastness, and (not least) the dramatic contrast they made against a simple unbleached muslin ground; their popularity has lasted well into this century.

Linens for quilt use seemed to have phased out as cotton fabrics became more plentiful after the turn of the nineteenth century, and woolens remained a quilt staple—even for quite elaborate quilts—until early in this century. Exotic silks were at a peak of popularity in the late 1870s and 1880s, in large part due to the Japanese and Chinese exhibits at the Philadelphia Centennial Exposition in 1876. A journal of the day noted that "silks are either brocaded or embroidered by hand... black and Bismarck grounds, are strewn with flowers of brilliant hues, half-blown roses, heather-bells, daisies, and convolvulus.... In plain colors, there is a novelty called joult de soie antique, a thick corded silk with the lustre of satin.... Another novelty is the chameleon, a revival of the changeable silks that take new tints in different lights."[34] The Victorian love of embellishment was reflected in these fabrics as well as in the heavily ornate Crazy quilts in which they often appeared.

Conventional wisdom holds that fabrics were fre-

86. Tumbling Blocks; Ella Mary Young Safford (1850–1924); Washington County; 1869–1870; pieced silk and taffeta; 75½″ x 69½″. Photograph by Sun and Sky Fine Fotos. (Collection of Dorothy Safford) This Tumbling Blocks quilt was made by the daughter of Louenza Clark Young, the maker of the Rising Sun quilt (see p. 63) when she was about nineteen or twenty years old, and she apparently learned her fine quiltmaking skills from her mother. The back of the quilt is pieced in a Nine Patch design, also in silks and taffetas. The less durable but more elegant fabrics such as silk, taffeta, and velvet were increasingly used in quilts at this time among the middle class, as quilts moved toward a decorative rather then utilitarian place in the household. In a letter in the possession of the present owner, a cousin in Westfield, New Jersey, wrote to Ella Mary on Mary 28, 1870, about the quilt: "Well, Ella, you said you had finished your silk quilt, and I should not wonder if you were glad, I know I would be, but I do not think mine will ever be finished…"

87. Ella Mary Young Safford

88. Wandering Foot; made by Harriet A. Jamerson Rowsom (1823–1905); Martinsburg, Lewis County; 1903; appliquéd cotton; 72″ x 72″. (Collection of H. Raynard Alger) Harriet A. Jamerson Rowsom married John Rowsom on December 28, 1841. She made this quilt when she was eighty years old and living in Martinsburg, Lewis County. The back is pieced out of sugar sacks, and she probably intended it to be used as a utility quilt. Cotton sacks have a long history of usage in quilts— particularly as backing—although their use tended to be more widespread in areas other than the Northeast. The current quilt owner is the great-grandson of the maker.

89. Rising Sun; made by Louenza Clark Young (1827–1884); North White Creek, Washington County; 1850; pieced and appliquéd cotton with stuffed work; 100″ x 94″. Photograph by Sun and Sky Fine Fotos. (Collection of Dorothy Safford) This quilt was made by Louenza Clark Young, possibly for her first child. The maker was twenty-three years old at the time and married to Robert Earl Young, the editor of the *Washington County Post*. Their child, Ella Mary Young Safford, was the grandmother of the present owner (see also p. 62). This quilt was meant to be a "special" quilt, for material had been specially purchased for its creation. Indeed, the maker made a list of the fabric costs: red material—$1.00, yellow—$.25, green—$.25, blue—$.25, white—$1.25, cotton (probably the stuffing)—$.31, and thread—$.38. Louenza Young was fully aware of the value of her time, for she listed that at $7.00. So the total cost of making the quilt was $10.69!

90. Louenza Clark Young and her husband, Robert Earl Young

quently recycled from clothing, curtains, tablecloths, or large pieces of bedding to carefully cut scraps for use in quilts and comforters; sometimes worn-out blankets or tattered quilts might even be used as batting for a new quilt. One theory for the lack of discovery of a large number of very early quilts is that cloth was at such a premium that it was continuously reused in this manner and would finally disappear from sheer wear and tear; another is that much of the scrap clothing and bedding of colonial times was used as rag for paper.[35] Fabrics in clothing surviving from the mid nineteenth century on often closely correspond to that of contemporary quilts of the period, substantiating the idea that dress scraps were almost always saved and used.

In addition to recycling clothing and other household fabrics, feed sacks were also recycled. During the course of the Project quilts from the late 1800s into the 1930s were seen that used feed sacks, either with the company logos still visible or just the plain areas, as backing. No identifiable cloth from dress-printed feed sacks was found in the tops or in the backs of the quilts reviewed, but this may have been partly a result of the higher cost of the printed sacks compared to the plain and partly due to the fact that some of the prints, once separated from their feed-sack origin, were so similar to other fabrics commercially available that they were difficult to discern.

There seems to be little doubt that many of the quilts registered during the Project were indeed scrap quilts— although many were clearly done with a certain aesthetic in mind, as the painstaking matching of hues and tones from a myriad of different prints would indicate—and there is no doubt either that a number of quilts had been created from fabrics bought specifically for a particular quilt. Each kind of quilt has its own brand of beauty and appeal, and even those among the most utilitarian of quilts seemed to have been made with the dual objectives of pleasing the eye of the beholder as well as of providing warmth.

91. Quilts are for more than beds. (Courtesy John Jackson Glass Negative Collection)

Images of Women

THE QUILTMAKERS OF NEW YORK
AND THE FORCES THAT SHAPED THEM

Quilting has been part of the history of New York for as long as there have been those who wanted warmth and comfort. The traditional skills and techniques of quilting in their homelands were part and parcel of the baggage that immigrants brought with them, but turns and twists in the thread of tradition occurred as adaptations were made to the resources and demands of the new environment. Thus, the form evolved—new, yet with elements of the traditional; familiar, yet constantly pressing the parameters of the known—always pushed forward by those who plied the needle and cut the cloth, for without the quiltmaker, the history of quilts could not exist.

And just who were the quiltmakers of New York State? Quilts, for the most part, have always been associated with women—women have been the primary makers, designers, purchasers, creators; their lives have often inextricably been tied to the fruits of their labor, and for so many years much of that labor hung on the skill of the needle. A brief glimpse into the lives of many of the makers of the New York quilts is offered in the captions accompanying the pictures of the quilts in this volume. However, all too often we know very little about the makers themselves, their lives, loves, aspirations, triumphs, and tragedies. Sometimes even their names elude us, and all that is left to recall a quiltmaker's life is the tangible and still-treasured product of her skill, the quilt.

Whether a quilt is a rote interpretation of a well-known pattern, a creative variation of what has gone before, or a flowering of innovative artistic expression, there is always within it a piece of the personality of the quiltmaker herself, the human factor that makes these objects more than a layer of warmth and color. Although every maker may not be known, we can look at the background and times that formed these women and the work they produced and gain some sense of who they were, what their lives were like through the records in thread as well as the diaries that they have left behind.

It is an interesting irony in history that the early colonial women had greater freedom and rights than would be the case for nearly the next two hundred years. However, the more liberal attitudes and the possibilities that they presented for women in those early days had already fallen by the wayside well before the Revolutionary War, as was indicated by Abigail Adams's plea to her husband to "Remember the Ladies, and be more generous and favourable to them than your ancestors."[1] Women's

92. Sunburst or Star of Bethlehem; made by Mary Catherine Davis Jones Woodhull (1827–1919); Miller Place, Suffolk County; c. 1843; pieced and appliquéd cotton; 90½" x 88". (Collection of Margaret D. Gass) Mary Catherine Davis, the maker of this quilt, wanted to marry her first cousin, Merritt Smith Woodhull, but their families felt they were too young. Woodhull shipped out on a clipper ship to China with the understanding that, when he returned, he and Mary Catherine would marry. During the two years of his absence, however, Mary Catherine married Benjamin Jones, a wealthy shipbuilder. Woodhull became captain of a sailing vessel and married a widow with two sons. In later years, after both had been widowed, Mary Catherine and Captain Woodhull finally married each other. Mary Catherine never had children of her own.

93. Rose of Sharon variation; made by Ann Butler Scutt (1813–1887); Livingstonville, Albany County; mid to late nineteenth century; appliquéd cotton; 75½″ x 80″. (Collection of New York State Museum, Albany, N.Y.) The maker of this elegant floral quilt was the daughter of the well-known tinsmith Aaron Butler. Butler, who operated a hay press, a cider mill, a brandy distillery, a decorating shop, a peddling business, and a farm in addition to his tinshop, taught his daughters to paint tinware. According to a grandniece, Ann was the one who did the most, and she had her own trade mark—a heart made of dotted lines, inside of which she painted her initials—that she would place on the pieces she painted. She went on business trips with her father to New York City and other places until her marriage to Eli Scutt in 1835. She decorated her new home with framed patterns done in the same manner as the tinware that she had painted.

94. Dome-top document box in painted tin; signed Ann Butler; c. 1830; Greenville, N.Y. (Collection of Museum of American Folk Art, New York City, 53.2.2)

participation in the broader avenues of everyday life was already well on the way to the middle-class constraints that demarcated their role in the nineteenth century.

From about the mid eighteenth century until 1940, the household—the woman's eminent domain—saw a major transformation in activities, functions, and needs. At the beginning of that era, women were still significant and crucial producers within the domestic setting—they not only dealt with the preparation of food and carried out other necessary chores, but they also supplied the clothing and bedding needs of their extended families, which might include servants, slaves, or hired help in addition to family members related by blood or marriage. By 1940, technological advances had wrought such changes in both the industrial and societal structure that women had moved to the opposite extreme—no longer was it necessary for the women of the household to be the primary producers of needed goods; the role of consumer was fully formed and the need for home production was completely negated.[2]

As life moved from an agrarian-based economy in which women could hold a place of full partnership in the economic family unit to an industrially based economy, one in which more and more men began to work outside of the immediate home unit at jobs that had no relation to a self-sufficient lifestyle, women were gradually forced into a subsidiary and limited partnership.[3] They had no part in the business world of their husbands; the husbands began to view the home as the background for their comfort. The home became a bastion of conservatism and an agency for social stability, and women took on the mantle of moral preceptor for the family. The latter part of the nineteenth century, a diverse age of romanticism, piety, and strict protocol, took its lead from the Victorian attitudes of England. All aspects of economic and social activity were subject to well-defined parameters, and women particularly were kept well-informed on the proper ways to conduct all aspects of their life through articles in the popular press and books on housekeeping, marriage, needlework, child rearing, and health. Fashion—and fads—were rigid and unbending, and many quilts of this period reflect the nineteenth-century woman's adherence to an unwritten social and cultural code.

This code extended to death as well as to all facets of life. Before the advent of modern health and medical practices in this century, death was a constant companion to the woman of the house, and in the nineteenth century the burden was particularly heavy. In addition to all her normal housewifely duties, she was expected to attend to all the necessary rituals of mourning when death occurred. This involved tokens of memorial sentiment, as well as special clothing, and there was no doubt that "the custom of mourning press[ed] far more heavily on women than men."[4] Mourning, especially in the second half of the nineteenth century, played a major part in the social life of the middle and upper classes; the poor could ill afford to indulge in the extravagances of the wealthier to acknowledge death and loss. Mourning customs had become institutionalized; books on manners, dress, activities, and the need to observe formalities abounded, and popular fiction often dealt with maudlin sentimentality and romanticized death.

Elaborate mourning rituals and remembrances reached their apogee after the mid-century mark, when Queen Victoria set a new standard for the world with her intense and dedicated prolonged mourning for her husband and her mother.[5] In this country, national mourning was at a peak following the assassination of President Lincoln, and notes from the diary of Caroline Dunstan of New York City give some indication of the response of the Union to the death of this singular man who had just seen his country through the bitter Civil War: "April 15, 1865. Margaret came to the bedroom door before 7 called me and told me that our great and good President Abraham Lincoln had been assassinated, shot last night by a wretch in the pay of northern traitors and southern rebels. Telegraphic communication from Washington states his death took place at 20 minutes past 7 this morning. . . . We put out our three largest flags draped in mourning, and hundreds of houses before an hour passed were covered with tokens of mourning." On April 18, 1865, her diary entry notes that "every house [was] in mourning" for the President.[6]

Mourning demanded changes in all areas of life, from bunting on the house to the family's wardrobe to the furnishings of everyday life. There were even stores in some of the larger towns that were devoted exclusively to the items needed to show respect for the dead, as is indicated in this entry from Dunstan's diary: "Sarah May and I at Jackson's Mourning Store bought mourning calico dresses for Mrs. G Mrs. H and Annie."[7]

It would not be unusual for a family with enough resources to dress their beds in white, gray, black, or black-bordered sheets, quilts, and blankets, just as they dressed themselves in those traditional colors of death. While earlier in the century verses were embroidered on samplers for presentation to the bereaved mourners, now quilts were occasionally used to memorialize the dead.

They might boldly remember the dead with stark lettering, or they might be made from the silks of a coffin or the ribbons from the wreaths sent in honor of the deceased, as were some examples seen during the Project. The clothing of the dead person might also be used as a means of remembering in a quilt made by a surviving relative, or by a group of people who wished to share their loss and their memories together. One quilt registered was made by a mother to pay the funeral expenses for her four children who had died of influenza, but her husband would not let her sell the finished piece.

One quilt seen apparently memorializes more than one person, as the blocks contain the names of a number of people from Dryden, Tompkins County, some of them related to one another. The green fabric separating the signature blocks is especially typical of this area of the state.[8] Many of the blocks have memorial verses written on them, often with a name, death date, and age. The verses were from moralistic or religious tracts, many of which had been used in earlier years as sources for the verses that appeared on samplers.[9]

> But death the early reaper, he
> Who ever plucks the fairest flowers
> Has been among us, Stolen the(e)
> And borne the(e) from this world of ours.
>   Almira Fitts, Died
>   October 8the 1842
>
>   C.C. Hurd
>   Died Oct
>   11the 1845
> She has gone to the mansion of rest,
> From a region of sorrow and pain
> To the glorious land of the blessed
> Where she never can suffer again.
>   Aged 25 years
>   1 month
>   7 days

Other blocks carry simply a name, sometimes with a town name and/or a date. However, the dates span more than half a century, from 1842 to 1902, presenting an intriguing problem for the researcher. It is not known whether the quilt was made in 1902, with some people memorializing relatives who had died earlier; whether it was made in the 1840s—most blocks date from 1846—with names and verses added over the years to blank blocks; or whether the quilt blocks were made in the 1840s and then put together closer to the turn of the century, again with the later maker adding some text of her/his own. An argument for the blocks having been made at the earlier date is the fabrics of which they are composed, all of which appear to date from prior to the mid nineteenth century.

In spite of the limitations that the evolving societal

95 and 95a. Sampler; made by Mary Catherine Dearborn Close (1832–1917); Katouah, Westchester County; 1847–1849; pieced and appliquéd cotton with stuffed work; 110″ x 90½″. (Collection of Helen H. Frisbie) Mary Catherine Dearborn married Ammi Keeler Close in 1853 and had two sons, Charles and Arthur. The quilt remained in the possession of Charles and his wife Johanna until their deaths, when it passed to the mother of the present quilt owner. Mary Catherine started the quilt when she was fifteen and finished it at seventeen. Although it includes many of the popular motifs of the times, there are some very personal touches, such as a depiction of the family home and the Columbia, a prototype for early steam engines. Her sashing is done in the form of daguerreotype frames and is most original. Mary Catherine was careful to include a "conventional" mistake in her link-chain around the horse by making one of the links red.

96. Mary Catherine Dearborn Close

95a. Detail

97. Crazy; made by Hessie Louise Walker Mohorter (1857–1926); Jordan, Onondaga County; 1884; cottons; 81″ x 78″. (Collection of Eunice M. Mohorter) Hessie Louise Walker Mohorter made this delightful Crazy quilt when she was twenty-seven years old. She embroidered it with farm animals, household articles, leaves, vegetables, and other naturalistic forms, all of which seem to relate to the way of life of the family of the quiltmaker. The present owner is the granddaughter of the maker.

98. Crazy; made by Josephine Cashman Hooker (1860–1912); New York City; 1880; velvet and satin; 48″ x 50″. (Collection of Margaret Hooker Kirkland Musil) The fabrics in this dazzling quilt, so typical of the late nineteenth century, are scraps from gowns created for the quilter. Obviously, she was a woman of leisure and means, one who could well afford luxurious fabrics. Josephine Cashman Hooker was raised in a mansion at the corner of Fifth Avenue and 32nd Street in New York City and educated at the Roberts School in New York and by private tutors; she also spent one year in Paris at Madame Mottets' school. She made several trips abroad with her mother, Honoria Elizabeth Cashman Hooker, who kept meticulous diaries of the trips, including notations of purchases of fabrics to decorate and furnish their home in New York, along with silks, lace, clothes, painted fans, and embroideries; it is probable that many of the fabrics in the quilt resulted from these trips to Europe. The quiltmaker was a direct descendant of the Reverend Thomas Hooker (1586–1647), a Congregational minister who founded Hartford, Connecticut, and whose sermon, "Fundamental Orders" (by which Connecticut was long governed), was the inspiration for the United States Constitution. The owner of the quilt is the granddaughter of the maker.

99. Josephine Cashman Hooker

100. Memorial for Nancy A. Butler; made by Nancy Ward Butler; Jamestown, Chautauqua County; 1842; pieced and appliquéd cotton, 79⅝″ x 80⅝″. (Collection of Smithsonian Institution, Washington, D.C.; Gift of Nancy A. Butler Werdell) This quilt was made to mark the death of Nancy Ward Butler's granddaughter, also named Nancy. The primary fabric is a roller-printed blue discharge print. The donor, a descendant of the maker, is also a namesake of this young woman whose life ended so abruptly.

101. Crazy; made by Barbara Strife Becker (1852–1946); Kirschnerville, Lewis County; 1883; pieced and embroidered wool, velvet, and taffeta; 87″ x 67″. (Collection of Theresa Birchenough) Four of the Beckers' thirteen children died of influenza within a short time of each other, and Barbara Becker intended to help pay their funeral expenses by making and selling this quilt. Her husband, however, refused to let her sell the quilt, saying that she worked too hard on it, so it has remained in the family through the years. The present owner is a granddaughter of the maker.

102. Chimney Sweep Memorial; makers' names unknown; Dryden, Tompkins County; 1846–1902; pieced cotton; 88″ x 70″. (Collection of Julie Clemens) The Chimney Sweep pattern was an extremely popular one for signature quilts as the large central cross in each block—usually made of unbleached muslin—provided an ideal space for an inscription, and this quilt makes good use of the space. It contains memorial verses, death dates, and a number of names; the recurrence of certain last names would seem to indicate that some were related.

104. Ella R. Hill Faatz

103. School House; made by Ella R. Hill Faatz (1849–1928); Weedsport, Cayuga County; c. 1916; pieced cotton; 78" x 76". (Collection of Virginia Faatz Hodock) This charming School House quilt was made by the present owner's grandmother. Family history notes that she made six identical quilts—one for each of her six grandchildren—but when an unexpected seventh grandchild came along, she did not want him to be slighted and therefore removed one strip from each of the six original quilts and put them together to make the seventh. (Presumably she had finished only the tops of the quilts and so found the task of altering them less arduous!) Ella Hill was born in Brutus, New York; she was married in 1870 to Lovius DeLacy Faatz in Sennett, New York, and they moved to Weedsport, where she was living when she made this quilt and where she later died.

structure placed on women, in some arenas opportunities and attitudes began to change and expand. The increasing leisure time that women might have had because of technological progress starting in the early 1800s gave impetus to an increase in literacy for women, and education became of greater importance than it had been in pre–Revolutionary War America.

The first school in New York had been established by the Dutch about 1633, and at the close of the Dutch dominion of the region there was a free elementary school in almost every settlement. The British government, however, did not consider the maintenance of schools to be a government duty, and education prior to the American Revolution became largely a private affair. The youngest children were taught at home or, if the families were more affluent, sent to dame schools, which taught the rudiments of reading, writing, and mathematics, and the curriculum for girls from the youngest ages on always included needlework. Older children were sent to private academies or seminaries for further schooling, and young women from wealthier families in the rural areas were often sent to finishing or boarding schools. The poor, whether boys or girls, received no formal education, other than what might be supplied in the home or by such church or charity schools as there were.

The ratio of boys to girls in the early schools was at least four to one; even the educational system in New Amsterdam (which was considered more liberal than the English system in educating girls) in the seventeenth century showed a preponderance of male students, although it had been noted that "the girls, though fewer in number, had learned and recited more than the boys."[10] It was not until the nineteenth century that the community as a whole began to believe that a girl needed "mental culture and acquirements" if she were to discharge her duties as wife and mother (as well as instructor and role model) appropriately.

The Revolutionary War disrupted such formal education as there was, but shortly after independence, Governor George Clinton, recognizing that educated citizens would be a major asset for the new nation, recommended that provision be made for educating the children of the state.[11] In 1784, the State Legislature formed the University of the State of New York, which had the power to charter secondary schools, and the Clinton Academy in East Hampton, Long Island, which

105. Teaching Quilt; made by Elizabeth Hamilton (d. 1950); probably Patchogue, Long Island; 1934; pieced and appliquéd cotton; 85″ x 80″. (Collection of Ruth G. Strong) This delightfully eccentric version of a teaching quilt was designed and made by Elizabeth Hamilton, a cousin, for the present owner to play on as a child so that she could learn her letters, numbers, and shapes. The initial "G" on all the jugs stands for the owner's family name, Grueschow. She recalls that "Cousin Lizzie, as she was reverently called, was in her sixties when she made the quilt. She resided near the bay in Patchogue, Long Island, and was a very artistic maiden lady. A spunky lady, her mode of transportation was always a bicycle." She also remembers "Cousin Lizzie spending Christmas at our home in Patchogue. She would recite *A Christmas Carol* faithfully for us, and this quilt was always placed around the base of our Christmas tree. After I married and had children, I continued this tradition, as I'm sure my daughter will do also."

claims to be the "oldest academical institution in the State of New York," was chartered in 1787. Support came from voluntary contributions, and students were expected to pay tuition; it was generally accepted that schools provided educational opportunities only for the children of the more prosperous citizens.

In 1795, the state legislature passed its first act to maintain and encourage "common schools" for elementary education. All children were to be instructed in the English language and arithmetic or mathematics and other subjects that were appropriate to the completion of a good education. Funds for the schools' maintenance were appropriated from local taxes, and districts were created to distribute these moneys, to determine the number of days of schooling, and to hire teachers.[12] There was, however, great unevenness at all levels in the state educational system until the twentieth century.

There was an increased interest in advanced education among the upper and newly emerging middle classes from the early nineteenth century on, and academies and seminaries became popular for schooling beyond the common school level. These institutions could be single-sex or coeducational, and many of them had close ties

(possibly stimulated by the religious zeal of the Second Great Awakening), financial and otherwise, to church denominations, underscoring the influence and importance of religion in these early years.[13]

The Troy Female Seminary, an all-girls' school founded in 1821 by Emma Willard, offered "genteel instruction in music, art, and other accomplishments suitable to a young lady of leisure."[14] The New York Conference Seminary, built in the tiny town of Charlotteville in Schoharie County in 1850, drew its students, both male and female, from far and wide. In the 1854–1855 school year it had a student body of 455 "ladies" and 798 "gentlemen" representing most of the states then in the Union as well as Cuba, Quebec, and Nova Scotia.[15] The school's catalogue listed twenty-five subjects, from Spanish and Italian to Latin and Greek, from guitar music and the making of wax fruits and flowers to mathematics and history. Unlike the Troy Female Seminary, the seminary in Charlotteville put a heavy emphasis on academic subjects; a course in ornamental needlework was offered, but students were levied an additional charge of $3.00 to take it.[16]

By the time of the Civil War, enrollment at many seminaries and academies in the state had decreased

106. Feathered Star or Sawtooth; made by Mathilda Onderdonk (1829–1900); Pomona, Rockland County; c. 1860; pieced cotton; 96″ x 70″. (Collection of Rachel Kaufmann) This quilt was made by Mathilda Onderdonk, who was born in Pomona, Rockland County. She is thought to have made the quilt sometime during the third quarter of the nineteenth century, and her name is cross-stitched in one of the center blocks of the quilt. An inventory of her estate valued her quilts at fifty cents each, and this striking red and white sawtooth quilt is one of those listed. Mathilda Onderdonk's family was of Dutch origin and were members of the Dutch Reformed Church, commonly called the "Brick Church," in West New Hempstead.

107. New York Conference Seminary, Charlotteville, New York. (Courtesy Anonymous Arts Recovery Society, Charlotteville Museum)

108. Star of Bethlehem; made by a member of the Cornell family; Ithaca, Tompkins County; c. 1880; pieced and appliquéd cotton; 94″ x 92″. (Collection of Judith and James Milne, Inc.) This vibrant Star gives a sense of optical illusion and movement. Oral tradition associates the quilt with the Cornell family, one of whom founded Cornell University in Ithaca. Ezra Cornell (1807–1874) began life as a laborer but, because of an ingenious mechanical bent and a shrewd business mind, he managed to become a millionaire by the end of the Civil War. He pursued a long-standing interest in agricultural education by pushing for legislation in the New York State senate to found an agricultural college in Ithaca, his hometown since 1828. After the United States Congress passed a law in 1862 to provide federal public lands to each of the states as an endowment for education in agriculture and the mechanical arts, he took advantage of the failure of a small agricultural college in the state and persuaded the state legislature to transfer the grant to Cornell University, which he founded in 1865.

substantially; the developing democratic philosophy in the country was then rejecting the exclusiveness of such schools and a movement had begun to make secondary education available to "all deserving pupils."[17] The growth of the public high school after the end of the Civil War saw a continuing decline in these private schools, and the heyday of the seminary drew to a close.

Colleges and other institutions of higher education had existed for men in New York since the early eighteenth century (Columbia University was established in 1754), but the state—like the rest of the country—was not forward in promoting higher education for women. The very first female college in the United States was chartered in Auburn, New York, in 1852 (it was transferred the next year to Elmira and later became the Elmira Female College); it was followed by Vassar in 1865. Coeducation in higher education did not exist until after the Civil War.

Whether public or private, free or costly, there was one area of agreement in education that remained constant through the years—girls needed to know how to sew. In the earlier days of colonization, sewing and needlework was considered at least as important—if not more so—than reading and writing for young girls. Certainly at one time in the state's history sewing, along with spinning and weaving, was a crucial skill if family members were to be regularly supplied with clothing and bedding. References to plain sewing and fine needlework abound in early diary entries, and children might learn to ply a needle at as early an age as two or three. It was expected that by age "nine or ten [a girl] should be doing her own mending, etc."[18] The New York Quilt Project registered some quilts made by children as young as five years old, underscoring the importance of the essential skill of sewing and the belief that it could not be learned too early.

Not every child, however, took kindly to the needle, as can be attested in both fact and fiction. Caroline Richards notes that "I am sewing a sheet over and over for Grandmother and she puts a pin in to show me my stint, before I can go out to play. I am always glad when I get to it";[19] Helen Doyle, another upstate resident, also noted the restriction on her childhood activities: "...every day I must sew one square of nine blocks before I am free to play."[20] And Mrs. N. H. Dayton of East Hampton recalled that when she was a child, her grandmother made her do a stint every day and that if it were not done well enough it would have to be done over; Mrs. Dayton says that she thought that "the quilts would never need washing, they had been soaked in tears enough to keep them clean for a lifetime."[21] Popular fiction also recognized the burden of the needle in a serialized story: "Orphelina was taught very early to sew, that she might make herself useful.... Many tedious hours did she pass seated on a stool at her needle, labouring to accomplish tasks that were always too long for a child of her age..." and later, in a quote from the heroine herself, "I know very well that all people ought to sew, else nobody would have clothes to wear; and I am willing to sew some part of every day. It may be very wicked to say so—but indeed Mrs. Kimberly almost makes me hate the sight of a needle."[22]

Girls were started on their sewing careers with samplers because they provided an opportunity to develop stitching skills without the risk of wrecking a usable

109. Detail of Mosaic variation; made by Carrie S. Norton (1869–1960); Sandy Creek, Oswego County; 1875; pieced cotton. (Private collection) Carrie Norton was only six years old when she completed this quilt, which, in spite of its simplicity, won her a prize—a picture of Red Riding Hood—at the Sandy Creek Fair in 1875. In 1982, the quilt won a blue ribbon at the Sandy Creek Fair—this time for being the oldest quilt in the show. The quilt is inscribed in dark woolen thread, "Made by Carrie Norton at age 6/Presented to Arrie Norton." Arrie was Carrie's brother. Carrie Norton's mother, Harriet M. Stokes Norton, was the milliner in Sandy Creek and taught her sewing skills to her daughter. Carrie grew up to marry F. Dudley Corse, the editor and publisher of *Sandy Creek News* from 1885 until his death in 1929. Carrie succeeded her husband as editor and publisher and served in that capacity until 1942, when William J. Potter, her daughter's husband, succeeded her. The present owner is the maker's daughter. She notes that the quilt has never been used and that the picture that Carrie won still hangs in her hallway.

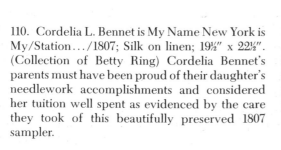

110. Cordelia L. Bennet is My Name New York is My/Station.../1807; Silk on linen; 19½″ x 22½″. (Collection of Betty Ring) Cordelia Bennet's parents must have been proud of their daughter's needlework accomplishments and considered her tuition well spent as evidenced by the care they took of this beautifully preserved 1807 sampler.

and sometimes expensive piece of fabric—that letters and ciphers were also learned through samplers was essentially secondary to the development of needlework techniques—and because they enabled a girl to learn the basic skills that defined an important economic role of the woman within the family. Additionally, childhood in the early years of the nation was not the carefree and exploratory period that is now regarded as natural; children, and particularly those in poor or less well-to-do families, were expected to contribute in one way or another to the maintenance of the family from an early age. Sewing was not only a practical skill that could serve the family well, it also could keep a child well-occupied for long periods while improving necessary skills. Very young boys often learned basic sewing as well as the girls, but they tended to give it up as soon as they were old enough or strong enough to begin taking on other chores around the house or farm, or, if from a wealthy enough family, to be sent for formal education in the more academic or "manly" subjects.

A girl's mother or another female relative might prove to be her first sewing teacher, but further opportunities for tuition were abundant as these examples from newspapers of the times indicate:

> "Lately arriv'd in this city from Great Britain, Mrs. Mary Gray, who professes teaching all sorts of Plain Work in the neatest manner...." (*The New-York Mercury*, October 8, 1753)

> "Mrs. Edwards, Lately from England, Begs leave to acquaint the Public, that she proposes opening a school and Boarding, for young Ladies...where will be taught Reading, all kinds of plain Work, Samplers...." (*The New-York Journal*, October 13, 1768)

Needlework was, of course, part of the curriculum of a young lady at almost any school in the state, and a young woman was expected to improve her skills in this area continually. The Reverend Lyman Beecher and his wife, Roxana Foote (parents of Harriet Beecher Stowe), had a "select school" in East Hampton where Roxana taught the higher English branches and French, drawing, painting, and embroidery. The importance of this latter subject is recalled by her sister, as she mentions "several large pieces of embroidery that were done by her scholars. Embroidery was an essential accomplishment then."[23] Hannah Helme, one of the signers of an album quilt registered during the Project, studied with Roxana Beecher and undoubtedly refined some of her needlework skills there. The amount of time spent on the subject is implicit in a letter written by Eliza Helme, Hannah's cousin, to her mother on October 4, 1806; she remarks that "Mrs. Beecher thinks if I work forenoon and afternoon I shall finish it [her embroidery] this quarter and I think I shall."

The ability to sew was also considered to be a prime requisite for marriage, and any girl who could not sew

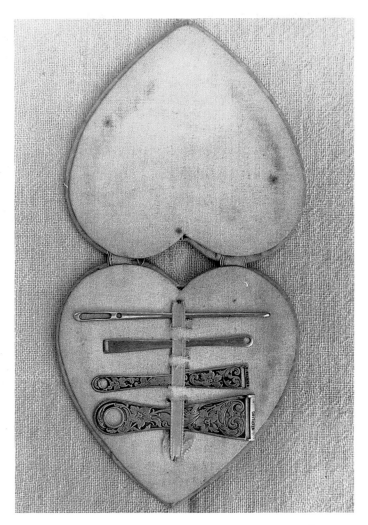

111. Ribbon bodkins in assorted sizes in ornamental silk cases were gifts appreciated by young women. These date around 1875. (Courtesy Dr. Suzanne Murphy)

would certainly be considered somewhat odd.[24] Articles reiterating the important requisites in a wife always noted that as part of her domestic duties she "ought to know how to sew, and knit, and mend, and cook and superintend a household,"[25] while *The Young Lady's Friend* in 1837 counseled young women to allot time for this important skill and to "have a piece of needlework always at hand."[26] A basic home reference made the unqualified statement that, "Every woman, rich or poor, should know how to use a needle neatly and swiftly."[27] Even those young women who sought and sometimes found alternatives to marriage and life as circumscribed by the traditional domestic sphere found sewing skills to be useful and necessary adjuncts to their social life, as sewing societies offered ideal opportunities for conversation and companionship.

The emphasis put on needlework skills for young women persisted well into the century, and even later.

112. Sampler Album; made by the Ladies of Mt. Sinai Church Group; Miller Place, Suffolk County; 1846–1847; pieced and appliquéd cotton; 97″ x 99″. (Collection of Margaret D. Gass) The Mt. Sinai Congregational Church serves the three towns of Mt. Sinai, Miller's Place (now corrupted to Miller Place), and Rocky Point, all contiguous and located on the north shore of Long Island. The quilt was made and sold for the benefit of the church. The center block of the quilt contains the following poem written in ink:

> Oh what of the land thou doest hover o'er,
> Bright bird of the tireless wing?
> Say is there no grief on what peaceful shore
> And blooms there eternal spring?

> From far away in my beautiful home,
> From all that to sin can entice,
> High o'er your earth and its sorrows I soar,
> I'm a bird of paradise.

It is signed by Hannah Helme Woodhull (1793–1857), the wife of General John Woodhull and sister-in-law to Caleb Smith Woodhull, mayor of New York City at the time of the Astor Place Riots. Mary Woodhull, another signer, was Hannah's sister-in-law and the mother of Captain Merritt Smith Woodhull, husband of Mary Catherine Davis Jones Woodhull, the quiltmaker of the Star of Bethlehem quilt on page 65.

The advent of new manufacturing technology and broader attitudes about the education of young women in the latter part of the nineteenth and early twentieth centuries eventually began to diminish interest in sewing skills, but the real seal on the demise of fine needlework as an intrinsic part of a girl's education may be attributed to the rise of the department store. With the expanding availability of ready-to-wear goods, the arduous labor required in the home production of clothing and bedding became less a matter of basic survival and more a matter of choice—and many women began to choose other outlets for their energies.

As much as a woman's needlework skills were, for so many years, signs of her dependent status and relegation to the domestic sphere, they have also served as something in which she could take great pride. Many women entered their handiwork in local and state fairs as a way first, perhaps, of establishing their skills as something of value and worth admiration, and second, as a means of bringing in a few extra well-earned dollars, for premiums of one to three dollars often accompanied the ribbon awards. The fairs, which provided an important recreational event for much of rural nineteenth-century America, established a precedent for handiwork competition among women and may have served as the forerunners of the quilt contests, such as the Sears Century of Progress contest, that began to blossom in this century.

Although the tradition of the English county fair, centered around sheepshearing and sales of horses and cattle, had been transplanted to Long Island as early as 1693,[28] the first documented fair in the United States was organized in 1810 by Elkanah Watson (sometimes known as the "father of the agricultural fair") in Pittsfield, Massachusetts.[29] This first fair was primarily an exhibition of livestock, but the principles espoused—judged exhibits, prizes awarded, and public display of entries—became basic to all future fairs.

Watson, who lived in Albany before and after his Pittsfield sojourn, helped to organize and promote New York's first fair, the Otsego County Fair held in Cooperstown in 1816. He recommended a range of activities at the fairs, and by 1819, the Schoharie County Fair, for example, was an impressive event, with bands, parades, pageantry, awards, and a gala ball concluding the festive day. The first State Fair, held in Syracuse in 1841, lasted two days and drew large crowds from miles around who were anxious to inspect the farm produce, livestock, and tools on display.[30]

Although the earliest fairs had focused mostly on agriculture, some also featured articles of domestic manufacture, which included quilts. The Elmira Fair in 1842 shows "Mrs. Hannah Wynkoop, then 65, receiving...two dollars for the best bed quilt, 'a beautiful article of domestic manufacture.'"[31] That quilts quickly became recognized as a significant part of domestic manufacture

113. This Adirondack-made spool holder with its storage compartment provided a compact and decorative place for sewing implements. (Courtesy Dr. Suzanne Murphy)

is highlighted by a comment in *The Cultivator* in 1844 on "...the many excellent specimens of quilts and other articles of domestic use and comfort conferring the highest credit on the truly worthy contributors."[32]

Singled out for special praise at the State Fair in 1846 was the "large collection of domestic and household articles made of silk, worsted, and other materials...rendered very interesting by the fact that they were produced from the farm of Dr. S. Voorhees, of Amsterdam and manufactured by his wife, the thread, floss, silk, etc. being all spun, wove, dyed, and manufactured by herself."[33] Mrs. Betsey Voorhees personified the educated nineteenth-century lady and her household skills. To her, needlework was an art form, indicating that some nineteenth-century women recognized their skills as being more than functional. She said in a letter to a cousin: "It [needlework] is in fact but a species of painting where the needle is used instead of the brush to diffuse the shade."[34] Mrs. Voorhees used the county and state fairs as well as the American Institute Fair in New York City as vehicles to display her needlework, and she won more premiums than any other woman in the state. At the 1847 State Fair, "the quantity and quality of [her] work...was so astonishing that the committee of judges awarded [her] a $10 premium and a silver medal.... This was an honor given to no other during the ten years that Betsey exhibited."[35] By this century, many fairs had

114. Whole Cloth; Mary Anna Hill McMinn (1826–1892); Davenport, Delaware County; March 24, 1859; cotton with stuffed work; 86″ x 78″. (Collection of Mrs. Donald Knowles) Mary A. McMinn lived in West Davenport, a small hamlet not far from Oneonta, and her family were sheep farmers. The owner, a great-granddaughter, says that the quiltmaker was thirty-three years old at the time the quilt was made. Mary Anna Hill was thirty-two when she married James McMinn on March 3, 1858; she had four children, three of whom died young. The following information is included in the quilt design: "Mary A. McMinn Davenport, March 24, 1859, M. F. Barstol, Artist." There are several touches of special interest in this quilt. An artist apparently was commissioned to draft the design, a pair of scissors is included below the central medallion, probably as a tribute to the maker's needlework skills, and a crowing rooster perches at the top of the central medallion. Family history states that the quilt was entered many times in the Old Oneonta Fair and always won first prize.

115. Grandma Moses, *Country Fair*, 1950, oil on canvas, 35″ x 45″. Copyright © 1989 by Grandma Moses Properties, Inc., New York.

116. Detail of a quilt made by Betsey Reynolds Voorhees. (Courtesy Montgomery County Historical Society, Fort Johnson, N.Y.) Betsey Reynolds Voorhees' skill as an award-winning needlewoman is attested to by this large white quilt with stuffed work made 1825–1840.

117. Baltimore-style Album; maker unknown; possibly East Bloomfield, Ontario County; 1845; appliquéd cotton; 99″ x 99″. (Collection of Mrs. Charles Zimmerman) This quilt was found in the family home in East Bloomfield, Ontario County, by the present owner after her mother-in-law's death in 1956. The quilt is dated 1845, and names on two of the blocks are Mary Foster and Elizabeth Holland, but they are unknown to the present owner. The quilt was probably made as a presentation gift or as a friendship offering, for an album quilt was a favorite format for this type of remembrance. The family exhibited this quilt at the Erie County Fair, where it was awarded the Tri-Color Award.

118 and 118a. Lady of the Lake; maker unknown; Germantown area, Columbia County; mid-1840s; pieced and appliquéd cotton with stuffed work; 92¾″ x 78″. (Private collection) This Lady of the Lake, one of the best examples of its type seen during the Project, was bought privately in Germantown by the present owner. It still had the yellow ribbon from a county fair on it as well as the entry ticket, showing that it had been entered in the antique-quilt category. No other information was available about the quilt, but the fabric and quilting techniques would point to the probability of a mid-1840s date.

119. *Annual Fair of the American Institute at Niblo's Garden*; c. 1845; watercolor drawing by B.J. Harrison; 20¼″ x 27½″; (Collection of Museum of the City of New York, 51.119; Gift of Mrs. J. Insley Blair) Quilts added to the colorful activity of the fair, and recognition of domestic-goods production as valid entries gave value to the fruits of women's labor.

instituted categories and prizes for the best antique quilts, and some of the quilts documented within this Project had been lovingly stored with their prize ribbons still attached.

As a counterpart to the state and county fairs, starting in 1828, New York City instituted an annual trade and technology fair sponsored by the American Institute that included exhibitors from across the country. The first notice of a prizewinning quilt at this fair came in 1843, under the general listing of "Shell Work, Waxed Flowers, Crimped Millinery, Corsets, Silk Embroidery and Samplers." A special category for quilts appeared in 1846, and in 1855, Andrew Blackwood of 104 Laurens Street won a diploma for an improved quilting frame, "a decided improvement."

From 1855 to 1858 the American Institute fairs were held at the spectacular Crystal Palace, located behind what is now the main branch of the New York Public Library at Fifth Avenue and 42nd Street and modeled after the famous iron, glass, and wood Crystal Palace in London. The New York Crystal Palace opened in 1853 with an international fair called "The Exhibition of the Industry of All Nations"; although well-attended, one contemporary critic noted that, "There was nothing of the least aesthetic interest except a few patchwork quilts, a trifling amount of fancywork, and an herbarium...."[36] The exposition did, however, serve as the prototype for the important Sanitary Fairs during the Civil War.

The industrial revolution in the textile industry may have moved the burden of cloth production out of the home, but women continued to sew their own clothes,

clothes for other members of the family, and bedding items as well as to mend and darn other articles. Even those families who could afford to hire outside seamstresses to help with the family's needs usually did part of the needlework themselves. Seamstresses very often did the cutting out of the patterns and the fittings but left the actual sewing of the garments or their embellishment with embroidery and the like to the women of the family. Quilts and bedspreads were almost always homemade affairs, even in the very wealthiest of families, although wealth would undoubtedly play a role in the lavishness or simplicity of the materials used.

For many a woman, sewing was a skill that might allow her to earn a respectable living in a time when few options outside of marriage or domestic household work were available. As one work of the time stated, "The needle has always been woman's legitimate weapon and ally. By it she has brought forth out of her treasures things new and old; she has warded off poverty from herself and family; has created much out of little; has for a lifetime rendered herself respectably independent."[37]

Sewing was among the few acceptable forms of employment for women in the eighteenth and early nineteenth centuries. Dressmakers, milliners, and some seamstresses were independent contractors; sometimes they had their own shops, sometimes they came and lived with a family during the period that it would take to get a season's wardrobe together.[38]

Seamstresses working in shop situations or at home on the "putting-out" system often did not find their lives easy; treatment and pay varied considerably from shop to shop, and shop employment, which often paid by the piece, sometimes seemed more like slave labor than a

120. A woman could open a millinery shop in her home and provide additional income for her family. (Courtesy John Jackson Glass Negative Collection)

83

121. Feathered Star; made by Lydia Brown Goff (1843–1925); Wellsville, Allegany County; 1865; pieced cotton; 80″ x 80″. (Collection of David A. Howe Library, Wellsville, New York) Lydia Brown Goff used some fine printed fabrics in constructing the quilt. Information given by the library states that the quilt took a year to make and that eleven spools of thread were used in the quilting (the common price for quilting at that time was $1.00 per spool). Lydia was born in Howard, Steuben County, and died in Wellsville, also in Steuben County.

good way to earn a living. Quilting was one way that women could earn extra money while working at home, and the work was often paid for by how many spools of thread were used rather than by the size of the quilt. One writer comments: "...those endless, endless stitches! [A woman] was paid, not for the amount of quilting she got through, but for the amount of thread she used, which may account for some of the amazing work on some of the old quilts. The way to beat that game was to take forty or fifty stitches to the inch!"[39]

The invention of the sewing machine brought about a dramatic change in women's lives in the mid nineteenth century. Although the amount of clothing and bedding needed was no less, women now had the advantage of a technology that could drastically cut the number of laborious, eye-aching hours that had been required to supply their families' needs. In spite of its initial cost, the sewing machine was rapidly and widely embraced by the women of America within a few years after Elias Howe's 1846 patent that became the prototype for later machines.

An article in an 1854 issue of the *Rural New-Yorker* noted that "about five years ago we do not believe there were more than three or four sewing machines in use in our country; now they can be counted by the thousands. They are to be found in the factories and in private dwellings, sewing the coarse bag and the most delicate piece of cambric."[40] Nor was there any doubt in people's minds about the labor-saving benefits of the new machine:

> A lady wishes to know if it will pay for our farmer's wives and daughters who have a good deal of work and but little help, to purchase Sewing Machines. It will pay well. With one of these machines the farmer's wife can do double the amount of sewing she has done in the old way with greater ease, and have enough time left to read books and papers, visit her friends, or help her poor neighbors. They are a great blessing for women, mentally and physically....we believe that while the men have reapers, mowers, etc., the women are entitled to labor-saving machines.[41]

By 1863 the sewing machine had become such an accepted item that the skills recommended and expected for a farm girl not only included cooking, milking cows, and making butter, cheese, and soap, but also knowing "how to use a sewing machine in a skillful manner."[42]

By 1856 Edward Clark, the partner of Isaac Singer (the recognized leader in American sewing-machine manufacture), had developed the concept of purchase on the installment plan. This notion brought the sewing machine within reach of a large number of women who might otherwise not have been able to afford them and, in many instances, gave those same women access to a new means of bringing in extra moneys to support their families as they began to take in piece work. Prices for machines also dropped dramatically, going from $125.00 each in 1850 (substantially more than cast-iron stoves—the major big-ticket item bought by mid-nineteenth-century consumers) to an average of about $64.00 by 1870.

Although many women continued to hand-stitch their quilts, the sewing machine proved a boon, particularly for piecing, and machine-stitched piecing quickly became ubiquitous. Appliquéing by machine was sometimes done, but it required a good deal more skill of the seamstress: "No doubt seamstresses found it difficult to control the three layers of top, batt, and lining while treadling the machine, for the working space was shallow, and the thread often broke. Once adept, however, some turned their attention to their fine quilts, where the visible stitch testified to their skill."[43] The quilt made by Mary Curry shows very skillful use of the sewing machine for appliqué. Although not the earliest machine-appliquéd quilt seen, few others showed such preciseness and good control of the machine. The more elaborate appliqué quilts for "special occasions" were, for the most part, still done by hand; still, one researcher estimates that at least ten percent of all the quilts made between 1865 and 1900 contain some machine appliqué or quilting.[44]

122. No contest! This Howe sewing-machine ad portrays the obvious advantages of a sewing machine over sewing by hand. (Courtesy The New-York Historical Society, New York City)

123. This horse-shape sewing machine may have made the housewife feel she could gallop through her sewing chores. (Courtesy Smithsonian Institution, Washington, D.C.)

124. Business card for the Singer Sewing Machine Company. (Courtesy The Historic New Orleans Collection, New Orleans, Louisiana) Isaac Singer's ability to advertise and promote his product for all types of sewing is demonstrated by this business card that reflects the fashion for making Crazy quilts in the 1880s.

125. Ocean Waves variation; Maria Jane Howell Billard (1843–1927); Peconic, Suffolk County; c. 1860s; pieced cotton; 80″ x 62″. (Collection of Lois B. Allen) An amazing number of different prints and solids went into this eye-dazzling quilt, yet the variety adds to the overall effect rather than detracting from the charm. The quilt is also an excellent example of the early use of a sewing machine for quilting. The maker was in her late twenties when she made the quilt, and it is assumed that it was made for utility. Maria Jane Howell was born, lived, and died in the village of Peconic on the north fork of Long Island; she came from a farming family, and her husband, Barnabus Billard, was a farmer and cabinetmaker. The present owner of the quilt is Maria's granddaughter.

126. Maria Jane Howell Billard

The advent of the sewing machine may have at first seemed like a godsend; by decreasing the domestic workload it seemed to offer opportunities for many women to be able to supplement their income while doing piece work at home, but in shop situations it only increased the pressure on the workers for higher output for little more pay. An 1867 issue of *Harper's Bazar* makes mention of "the poor sewing-girls.... Some of them have fallen into the clutches of the hard-hearted and grasping and are to be pitied. They are expected to be honest, faithful, prompt, and perfect in their work for a mere pittance."[45] Textile mills absorbed a great many young women from rural areas, while in the cities work was readily available for those with good sewing skills, giving many women a chance to establish an independent income, and girls flocked to the jobs. Shops expanded into factories, and the extent of the work led to the establishment in New York City of the first women's trade union in 1825, when local women employed in the needle trades organized.[46] This movement led to the formation of the Female Industrial Association, also in New York City, in 1845. By the mid-1800s, the number of women working in collar and shirt factories was so great that Kate Mullaney, a factory worker in Rensselaer County, organized the first nationwide women's union in 1864.[47] It was only natural for women to organize around their sewing skills as an evolution from neighborly quilting bees and church sewing societies.

As technological progress created more opportunities for women to work outside the home and women began to move enthusiastically into the shallower waters of the economic mainstream, they also began to articulate their discontent with existing laws and customs that discriminated against their sex. As America was the first country to have a representative government by men, it was to be expected that it would be the first in which women would ask for representation. By the early nineteenth century demands began to be heard on a large scale, and New York State led the way by having the first women's-rights convention, passing the first bill permitting women to own property, enacting marriage laws permitting divorce, chartering the first college for women, and

127. Basket of Tulips; made by Mary Armstrong Curry (1845–1921); Grahamsville, Sullivan County; 1876; appliquéd cotton; 91″ x 79″. (Collection of Mary Eldridge) Birds, rabbits, horses, cats, and a pig admire the flowers in this quilt that was made by Mary A. Curry for her only child, George. A sewing machine was used in the appliqué work on the quilt, and the excellent work shows how skilled Curry was with her machine. The date 1876 and the maker's initials are quilted in one of the blocks. George Curry died before 1889, at the age of twenty. The present owner is the great-niece of the quiltmaker, to whom Mary Curry willed the quilt upon her death in 1921.

128. Mary Armstrong Curry

129. Shirt-factory workers. (Courtesy John Jackson Glass Negative Collection) The development of clothing factories gave women an opportunity to move their sewing skills from the home into the commercial arena.

130. Flatbush branch of the Women's Needlework Guild. (Courtesy Brooklyn Historical Society) Sewing societies provided social fellowship, transmittal of needlework skills, and opportunities to do charitable work.

providing the leaders for the national movement for women's rights, Elizabeth Cady Stanton and Susan B. Anthony.

Stanton's 1848 convention in Seneca Falls to discuss "the social, civil and religious condition and rights of women" resulted in a Declaration of Sentiments and Resolutions that presented a comprehensive case for women's rights that comprised nearly every demand made for women in the ensuing years. The convention had far-reaching consequences, for not only were women concerned with securing legal and political rights for themselves, they also sought moral reforms such as temperance and the abolition of slavery.

Susan B. Anthony entered public life through her work for the temperance movement. After being denied an opportunity to speak at a temperance meeting sponsored by men, she helped organize the Women's State Temperance Convention of New York, the first convention of its kind, in Rochester in 1852. At about this time, Anthony and Stanton met and a lifelong alliance was forged. The temperance movement and the women's-rights movement then continued in tandem because the same persons were in the leadership. However, opposition arose from the more conservative elements of the temperance movement who were not in accord with the objectives of the women's-rights movement and did not like linking the two, and the Women's State Temperance Society ended a few years later, not to be re-formed for another twenty years.

In spite of this failure, organized work for women's rights began to take a definite shape in the state. The first large-scale event was the Woman's Rights Convention, held in Syracuse in 1852, and it was there that Anthony began her fifty-four-year leadership of the movement. Anthony, who saw no contradiction in domestic chores being done by women who wanted the vote, found it efficacious to take her message—whether temperance or women's rights—to women as they gathered together to quilt.[48]

The outbreak of the Civil War temporarily banished the issue of women's rights from public thought, but it resurfaced almost immediately once the war was over. There was an initial effort to join together rights issues for both women and blacks through the Equal Rights Association, but some of the issues and injustices were seen as too diverse. In 1869 the National Woman Suffrage Association was formed, with the object of obtaining a constitutional amendment to enfranchise women. The movement finally gained full rights for women in New York State in 1917, and in the nation in 1920—the same year that the eighteenth amendment to the Constitution (the Volstead Act), which forbade "intoxicating liquors," became law. Although the lack of receptivity to Prohibition by the general populace led to the repeal of the amendment in 1933, temperance sentiment remained

131. Suffragettes announcing a meeting. (Courtesy John Jackson Glass Negative Collection)

strong for a number of years, and a fundraiser quilt made by a WCTU chapter in Tompkins County in 1939 was registered during the Quilt Project.

The religious revival of the nineteenth century as well as the temperance movement actually worked to give women more power within a somewhat limited sphere, as such power continued to be tied overall to the concept of feminine responsibility for the moral guardianship of the family (and temperance was seen as a part of this guardianship). The surge of growth in missionary societies—of whatever denomination—during the Second Great Awakening provided women the opportunity to play an active role in at least the religious structure of the country. They now had the chance to influence the church establishment in a tangible way, and the societies, often organized, managed, and maintained by women, became prime vehicles for fundraising activities and, as such, of great importance to the churches. The missionary societies, along with ladies'-aid and auxiliary societies, helped to provide funds for home-church needs as well as missionary work, and a favorite source of revenue for these groups was the fundraising or subscription quilt, of which many were seen during the course of the New York Quilt Project.

Not only did the quilts raise money for the church or society, they also provided the opportunity for women to gather together for a bit of social interchange and relaxation, and all under the banner of "doing good"! The 1848 records of the Southold Ladies Sewing Society of the First Universalist Church note that, "We have made and quilted a comforter for the town poor, for which we shall be paid, by the town, $1.00," and further that, "the primary objective of our Society is to aid in deferring the expenses of the

132. Garden of Eden; made by Olive Newton Sheffer (1846-1918); Mechanicsville, Saratoga County; date unknown; pieced and appliquéd cotton; 79″ x 68″. (Collection of Carol L. Mackay) Olive Newton Sheffer joined her love of creating with fabrics to her interest in biblical stories to compose this original interpretation of portions of the Old Testament, beginning with Adam and Eve at the center. She was married on August 8, 1864, and for many years she and her husband made their home in Mechanicsville, New York. Before she became crippled with rheumatoid arthritis, she used to enjoy taking the trolley to Troy to shop. Troy in the early part of this century was a center of shirt manufacturing and a good place to pick shirt scraps for quilts; none of the fabrics in this quilt appear to be shirting fabrics, however, and it more likely dates from an earlier period in the maker's life. Note the plain borders at top and bottom; the fabric and stitching differ from the body of the quilt, and it is possible that these were later additions intended to lengthen the quilt to fit a larger bed.

133. Olive Newton Sheffer

church. The second is to promote the social interests of its members and friends."[49]

Another type of church-generated quilt that was—and still is—popular was the presentation quilt, or one made by the women of a congregation as a gift for the minister or his wife in recognition of the esteem in which he or she was held. The more elaborate of these generally featured decorative appliquéd album-type blocks, each produced by a different woman, that were then sewn together and quilted at a quilting bee at the church or the home of a member of the congregation. The blocks might depict popular patterns of the day, the church itself, or verses from scripture. Some served a dual purpose, with mem-

bers paying to have their names inscribed on the quilt in thread or ink, and the finished product then being presented to the minister along with the money raised for the church.

That sewing and quilting were important and integral parts of the religious life as well as the social life of the women in New York is evident in scanning the records of church societies and women's diaries of the times. The Southold records referred to above, for example, contain many entries over the years to sewing for friends and charitable causes and to raising money through sewing, and the diary of Caroline Dunstan has numerous references to sewing, bible society meetings, and going to

134. The Pieties Quilt; made by Maria Cadman Hubbard (b. 1769); probably New York State; 1848; pieced cotton; 88½" x 81½". (Collection of Museum of American Folk Art, 1984. 27.1; Gift of Cyril Irwin Nelson in loving memory of his parents, Cyril Arthur and Elise Macy Nelson) The inscriptions on this quilt are worked in an unusual pieced lettering technique and cover a full spectrum of homilies from "Be still and know that I am God" to "If you cannot be a golden pippin, don't turn crabapple." The quilt carries the name and age (79) of the maker and the year it was created (1848). Because of the extensive research that has been done on this piece by the Museum staff and students at the Museum's Folk Art Institute, the quilt, formerly attributed to New England, is now thought to have been made in New York. Maria Cadman Hubbard is a descendant of Edward Cadman, who settled in Austerlitz, Columbia County.

135. Dresden Plate variation; made by members of the Cardus Class of West Avenue United Methodist Church; Rochester, Monroe County; 1915–1920; pieced and appliquéd silk and taffeta; 77″ x 76″. (Collection of West Avenue United Methodist Church) The Cardus Class was the Sunday School class of the West Avenue United Methodist Church. More than 200 signatures appear on the quilt, and it is probable that each signer paid a fee to have her or his name included, thus helping to raise money for the church.

136. Crazy; made by The Ladies Aid Society, First Presbyterian Church; New York City; c. 1891; appliquéd and embroidered satin and silk; 106⅝″ x 107¼″. (Collection of Smithsonian Institution, Washington, D.C.; Gift of Emilie Noakes Manley in memory of Margaret Clarke Goodall Bradley, Mr. Manley's grandmother) This quilt has American patriotic motifs along with the flags of forty-eight nations and the signatures of President Benjamin Harrison and members of his cabinet on the circle of red and white stripes in the center. Signatures of state governors and inscriptions of G.A.R. units are also included. The quilt was made as a fundraising project by the ladies of the church on West 12th Street and raffled; it was then given to Margaret Clarke Goodall Bradley because of her work on the project, although she had not won the raffle.

136a. Detail showing the Brooklyn Bridge (completed in 1886) which is featured in the top border of the quilt.

137. Presentation; made by members of the Pleasant Valley M. E. Church, Dutchess County; c. 1938; cotton, muslin; 80″ x 66″. (Collection of Jacqueline M. and Edward G. Atkins) When this very simple signature quilt was purchased at a rummage sale of the North Blenheim Methodist Church in Schoharie County, the present owner was told that it had belonged to the wife of a former minister of the church and had been given to her by members of her church. The minister, W. R. Phinney, had served churches in the Poughkeepsie District in the 1930s, and the information embroidered on the quilt indicates that his wife, Florence, had been a member of the Pleasant Valley Church in the Poughkeepsie District. The center block of the quilt details the history of that church, from its origin in 1780 through an 1862 "shakeup" to the calm notation "Still unchanged 1938." After his retirement, the Reverend and Mrs. Phinney moved to the Blenheim area, where he worked with the church there. When Florence Phinney died in 1977, many of her belongings were given to the church to supplement its annual rummage sale.

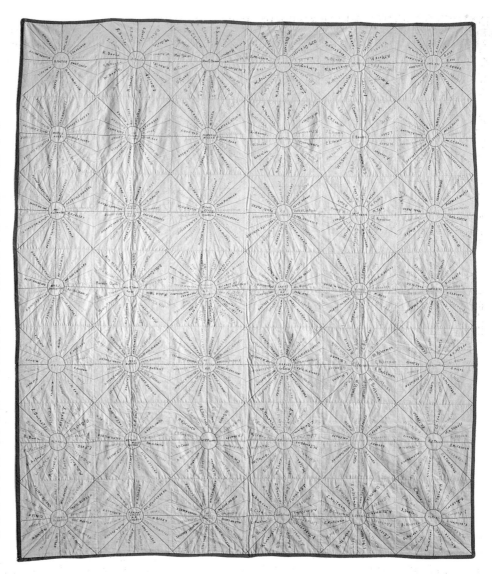

the "mission sewing school."[50] These same documents make it clear, however, that sewing societies not only promoted charitable deeds and fellowship but also played their part in continuing to teach the skills that were thought to be appropriate for women.

The ties between quilting, church work, and fundraising were firmly grounded by the end of the nineteenth century and continued well into the twentieth century. Today, even though the numbers of ladies'-aid and auxiliary groups—as well as their importance—have dramatically diminished, the ties between church and quilting remain strong, particularly in rural areas, as many women still use the church as a central gathering place for quilting together.

Throughout the years of women's history, sewing has, in many ways, been the connecting and common thread. Of all the skills that women have developed, it is the one that cuts across class, education, economic position, religious beliefs, and more. It has been the tie that binds, creating function as well as pleasure, and nowhere is its importance—and its capacity for creativity—more evident than in the quilts of the women of New York.

138. Presentation Sampler; made by Ladies of the West New Hempstead Reformed Church ("Brick Church"); Spring Valley, Rockland County; c. 1862; pieced and appliquéd cotton; 81″ x 88″. (Collection of West New Hempstead Reformed Church) This presentation sampler quilt was made during the pastorate of the Reverend Peter Allen, which lasted from 1837 to 1862 (a period of religious upheaval and dissension between traditional and modern voices), and presented to him upon his leaving the church. It descended in the family and was donated to the church, where it is now displayed, by Mrs. Samuel Gilner. The names of the quiltmakers, all members of the congregation, are inscribed on the blocks; one block was made by Mathilda Onderdonk, maker of the red and white Feathered Star quilt shown on page 74.

139. The Reverend Peter Allen, pastor of the West New Hempstead Reformed Church.

140. Floral Wreaths; made by Mary (b. 1830) and Deborah Palmer; Unadilla Center, Otsego County; mid nineteenth century; appliquéd cotton with stuffed work; 89″ x 92⅜″. (Collection of Smithsonian Institution, Washington, D.C.; Gift of Mr. and Mrs. Kenneth H. Hotchkiss) This quilt was designed by Mary Palmer and made by her and her sister, Deborah, and the workmanship is extraordinary. The delicate appliquéd rose petals, buds, and leaves are padded with stuffing worked in from the back of the quilt through slashes in the ground fabric; these cuts do not show, however, because they are hidden by the lining. The stems are made of green cotton wrapped around a thin roll of white cotton cloth. The whitework basket in the center and two grapevine wreaths that alternate with the rose wreaths were underlaid with cloth, quilted, and then stuffed through the layer of cloth from the back; the excess cloth was cut away at its outer edges.

141. Mary Palmer

142. Deborah Palmer

143. Original Design; made by Carl Klenicke; Corning, Steuben County; c. 1900; pieced silk, faille, taffeta, and satin; 72½″ x 60″. (Collection of Bessie P. Holmes) Carl Klenicke, a native of Germany, was a tailor in Corning. He made this spectacularly different quilt for his daughter, Laura (born in 1879), and son-in-law, Joseph Stenger, as a wedding gift. The design is wonderfully original, with folk motifs galore. It is a tour de force of pieced work, and it probably was made from scraps left over from the fabrics used in making clothes for his clients. The present owner of the quilt is Joseph Stenger's niece, and she inherited it from her mother, Helen Stenger Dolley, Joseph's sister.

Not for Women Only

Quilting is traditionally tied to the woman's domain, and the stereotypic image of a quiltmaker is that of a woman. Research, however, as well as the results of the Quilt Days, clearly showed that women did not have the field to themselves in New York State. A perusal of the reports of the state, county, and American Institute fairs revealed a number of men's names under the premiums awarded for outstanding quilts, but there is some question as to whether the men actually made the quilts themselves or were, perhaps, simply entering quilts that they happened to own and that had actually been made by women in their family or by a professional seamstress. (This same question holds true for premiums won by women as well, for very few of the reports actually specify that a quilt was "made by," only that a premium was "awarded to.")

A surprising number of quilts made by men turned up during the registration process, some of them being among the most original in terms of design and execution. The men responsible for the most outstanding of these were tailors, and perhaps quilting was simply an extension of their everyday craft that allowed for a greater degree of creativity than could be expressed in the conservative men's clothing of their times. In most cases, these quilts were made when the men were in their later years, and they may have felt that they were at a stage in their lives when they could afford some time for whimsicality and experimentation. Only Anthony Klem is known to have had some help with his quilt; his daughter, Theckla, helped with the tufting and buttons and referred to the quilt several times in her diary:

"Sept. 22, 1918: Went to Papa's [store] and saw quilt....

Nov. 24, 1918: Sat...upstairs watching Papa tie that quilt.

Dec. 15, 1918: Papa better—working on quilt.

Jan. 19, 1919: Papa upstairs working on my quilt.

Feb. 2, 1919: Papa and I made 26 bunches [tufts] on quilt. He got tired and I made them until train time, making 41 in all.

Feb. 9, 1919: Papa set me to work and he went in shop....I sewed on quilt until train time. I made 60 tufts. Left 11:15.

Feb. 23, 1919: I worked all a.m. on quilt and tied 50 until dinner time.... Tied 25 more until 6:30.

March 9, 1919: Lighted oil stove in Lillian's room and dried hair while I worked on quilt.... Worked on quilt until 6:30, making in all 50 pushels [tufts].... Mama thinks I'm such a good girl—so good to Papa.

March 23, 1919: Papa to store and I to the quilt. Papa had it all done but 36. Finished it with the exception of one button Papa had to make.... I sewed on button. Quilt done.... Home and train 11:15."

The quilts of the three men shown here reflect their profession in the materials used—silk and satin lining fabrics, suiting wools, buttons for trim, and so forth—but the sensibility of expression was uniquely their own and produced some of the most exciting images seen.

There were also quilts made by men for recreation, for therapy (such as a penny-square quilt composed of embroidered sports figures and scenes, made by an athlete recovering from an injury), or simply for everyday use. It was also discovered that a man was the oldest of the makers of any piece registered during the entire project—an unquilted top seen at the Niagara Quilt Day was the handiwork of a 100-year-old!

144. Original Geometric; made by Anthony J. Klem (1852–1921); Owego, Tioga County; 1914–1919; pieced wool; 78″ x 70″. (Collection of Jeannette C. Lee) Anthony J. Klem, a tailor, emigrated to the United States from Germany, where he had studied his craft. When he was in his sixties he made this quilt for his daughter, Theckla Klem Clark, a professional pianist in theaters, who also helped Klem tie the tufts on the quilt. He designed it himself, and it is made from scraps from his tailoring business, decorated with satin buttons, and tied with woolen tufts. According to the present owner, the granddaughter of the maker, Anthony Klem was the mayor of Owego in 1914.

145. Anthony J. Klem in his tailor shop.

146. Crazy; made by Job Mapes (1813–1905); Orange County; 1890; silk and velvet; 79″ x 69″. (Collection of Roger E. Frame) In addition to signing his name and the date, Job Mapes included his age—seventy-eight—on this quilt. The Mapes family were among the earliest settlers in Orange County and owned a farm in Mt. Hope; Mapes himself was a tailor by trade and clearly had access to many fine fabrics. He also had other skills, to judge by the embroidery and hand-painted leaves in the quilt. The present owner is a great-great-great-nephew of the quiltmaker, and his mother supplied much of the information that is known about Job Mapes. She recalled that he was a dynamic person and a family favorite about whom many stories are told.

147. Job Mapes

148. Original design; maker unknown; Albany area; c. 1900; appliquéd cotton with stuffed work; 79" x 75". (Collection of New York State Museum, Albany, N.Y.) This lively and idiosyncratic design has been nicknamed "Funky Chicken" by the museum's staff, for it seemed to resemble no other known design. The donor of the quilt could trace its ownership to her husbands grandmother, who lived in the Albany area at the turn of the century, but there was no positive evidence that she was the maker.

Images in the Making

COMMONALTIES, CONVERGENCES, AND CONTRADICTIONS IN NEW YORK QUILTS

One of the joys of an adventure such as the New York Quilt Project is the thrill of the hunt—one is never sure just what new and exciting patterns and designs will turn up—in addition to renewing acquaintances with many old favorites. In travels around the state during the documentation days, some facts became apparent from the sampling. All the quilt patterns that are so familiar to us today were represented in the quilts seen, as well as many original variations on a recognized theme; idiosyncratic and unique designs to which no known names may be ascribed also appeared with some regularity. Many times the documentors used pattern names familiar to their locale that might not be recognized elsewhere. Some patterns expected to be common were seen seldom or not at all. To our surprise, the New York Beauty pattern, for example, turned up infrequently; was this because the quiltmakers of the state found it of little or no interest, or was it simply a matter of the sampling process, and somewhere out there hidden in trunks, drawers, and closets are many New York Beauties waiting their chance for the limelight?

No quilt pattern or design over another could be said to typify the state, and although some types were seen more frequently in one locale over another, again, none could be said to be overwhelmingly representative of an area. Although no strong regional styles could really be identified among the more than 6,000 quilts reviewed during the Project, an interesting side note is the fact that the two quilts with the greatest number of pieces were both brought in on the same day, came from the same area, and were made roughly in the same period. These two quilts, each of which contained well over 20,000 pieces, were variations on the Broken Dishes pattern and were carefully made scrap quilts. One, shown on page 15, was made by the wife of a barge captain on the Erie Canal; little is known about the maker of the other. Several other quilts containing pieces in the thousands were also seen from this area, but none there or elsewhere matched these two for sheer numbers. One may speculate whether a short-lived fad for such quilts suddenly took hold in this area, or

whether the two quilts represent some sort of unspoken competition between two quiltmakers who quite possibly knew each other.

More Crazy quilts were registered than any other single kind of quilt, but the variation possible in the Crazy design makes each one almost a unique case. The most favored patterns of New York quiltmakers by virtue of numbers seen are in descending order: Stars (single and multiple), Log Cabin, Basket, Grandmother's Flower Garden, Chimney Sweep (with and without signatures), Irish Chain, Dresden Plate, Nine Patch, One Patch, Penny Squares, Whole Cloth, Double Wedding Ring, Flying Geese, Four Patch, Lady of the Lake, Bow Tie, Grandmother's Fan, and Tumbling Blocks.

Many times the quiltmaker had ascribed no name to her quilt, or the owner knew no name, and so various basic books served as the source in which a pattern's name might be found. Many patterns seemed familiar on first glance, but individual variations often made it more difficult to find an exact pigeonhole for some quilts. It is, in fact, precisely this possibility of taking the familiar and restructuring it into the new and different that lends quiltmaking its beauty and charm. In cases where a pattern might have more than one name (for example, a single-star quilt might be called Star, Star of Bethlehem, or Lone Star) or a very regional or local name, the name given by the maker or owner would be used and name variations also recorded.

The origins and names of some of the patterns are reasonably well established, but others still retain some ambiguity and may never be fully pinpointed. To give only a few examples: Star patterns, one of the most commonly seen in the project, are thought to be among the earliest of the pieced work and have been seen on quilts from 1775.[1] Basket patterns probably grew out of the earlier Medallion quilts or even quilting patterns, some of the more elaborate of which might show intricately stitched baskets brim-full of flowers, vines, or sometimes fruit. The pieced basket began to be seen around 1850 and has been a pattern of continuous

149. Rising Star variation; made by Elsey A. Halstead (1830–1850); Minisink (now Middletown), Orange County; March 23, 1848; pieced and appliquéd cotton; 100″ x 85″. (Collection of Margaret Halstead Minch) This splendid variation on a Rising Star pattern gains additional power from the bold pine-tree border. In an unusual touch, the maker has appliquéd pine cones, which have long been regarded as symbols of fertility, on the trees. Elsey A. Halstead cross-stitched her name, date, and the town in which she lived in red thread in a corner of the quilt, but she left no explanation for her design. The present owner of the quilt is her great-great-niece.

popularity ever since.[2] Grandmother's Flower Garden, also known as Honeycomb, Hexagon, or Mosaic, dates back to the early nineteenth century; the January 1835 *Lady's Book* notes that: "Patchwork may be made in various forms as stars, triangles, diamonds, waves, stripes, squares &c. . . . [but] Perhaps there is no patchwork that is prettier or more ingenious than the hexagon or six-sided; this is also called honey-comb patch work."

Stars in all their variations were among the most prevalent of the patterns seen, and they ranged from the single majestic star that dominated the quilt to repetitive blocks featuring stars with eight points or more. As the examples here and elsewhere in the book indicate, the star design is always striking in its impact and is well worth the effort required in stitching its precise points. Stars were a consistent pattern seen from the earliest quilts through the most recent, and their variety seemed limited only by the stretch of the imagination of the makers themselves. Although the use of the large single star (Star of Bethle-

hem or Lone Star) seemed to lose some of its popularity during the latter part of the nineteenth century, the turn-of-the-century revival of interest in traditional patchwork found the *Ladies' Home Journal* noting that it was one of "the most aesthetic patterns of the olden time, still it may be new to many of the rising generation."[3] Whether or not this article was the motivating factor, many single star quilts made between 1900 and 1930 were registered during the Quilt Days.

Variations on Basket designs turned up in every region of the state in significant numbers. As already noted, the Basket has long seemed to be a popular motif, from the early elaborate Broderie Perse examples that feature elegant baskets overflowing with flowers to the simple pieced geometric blocks that present an abstract view of this everyday item and that continue to persist as a favorite design. Some have speculated that the prevalence of baskets in design is related to the importance of baskets in everyday life—and particularly to the quilter's

150. Crazy; made by Florence Stevens Remington Penfield (1853–1935); Albany; c. 1880; silk and velvet; 77" x 65½". Photograph by Biff Henrich. (Collection of Mrs. Donald Coons) Florence Stevens Remington Penfield was the wife of Lamartine "Mart" Remington, the uncle of Frederic Remington, the artist. Frederic Remington withdrew from Yale College on the death of his father and came to stay with his uncle in Albany for three years. "Mart" was only thirteen years older than Remington but an important figure in Republican politics at the time. He found Remington a position as an executive clerk in the chambers of Governor Alonzo B. Cornell (the son of Ezra Cornell, founder of Cornell University). Remington hated the job but stayed on because of a romantic attachment to Eva Caten, whom he eventually married.

Frederic Remington painted pictures on several of the blocks of this Crazy quilt. In addition to his paintings, the quilt contains blocks made of small pieces of family clothing. The quilt was given to the mother of the current owner by Pierre Remington, son of Florence and "Mart," as a wedding gift.

151. Frederic Remington loved painting soldiers, two of which are seen in this detail from the quilt. In a letter to a fellow artist, Scott Turner, he wrote, "Your favorite subject is soldiers. So is mine." (From Peggy and Harold Samuels, *Frederic Remington: A Biography* [Garden City, N.Y.: Doubleday & Co., Inc., 1982], 21.)

152. Grandmother's Flower Garden; made by Leila Kuhl Briggs (1890–1982); Presho, Steuben County; c. 1900; pieced cotton; 92" x 83". (Collection of Karna E. Kuhl Palermo) Grandmother's Flower Garden was a favorite pattern of young quilters at the turn of the century, and Leila Kuhl Briggs was no exception; she was only about ten or eleven years of age when she made this quilt. Leila was raised on a farm in the area, and the present owner is her niece.

153. Star; made by Emily Webb Fosdick; Monroe, Orange County; c. 1854; pieced cotton; 92" x 76". (Collection of Phyllis Klein) This quilt was purchased by the current owner from Elizabeth Mapes Whiteheart, the great-granddaughter of the quiltmaker. Emily Fosdick's family has resided in Orange County for many generations and has ties by marriage to many other long-time Orange County families.

154. Touching Stars; made by Eliza Kittle Russell, Harriet Rogers Russell, and other family members; Stephentown, Rensselaer County; c. 1850s; pieced cotton; 87″ x 68″. Photograph by Fred Ricard. (Collection of Helen P. Vedder) This quilt was believed to have been made at the Russell family farm. The Russells attended the Baptist Church in Stephentown where, according to diaries and other books in the State Museum in Albany, many quilting bees were held. Mrs. Vedder, the present owner, is the great-granddaughter of Eliza Kittle Russell on her father's side.

155. Cherry Basket; made by Dora Stevens Rush (1847–1887); Camden, Oneida County; 1868; pieced cotton; 79″ x 69″. (Collection of Constance M. Kelley) There are 195 miniature baskets in this charming quilt made by the great-great-grandmother of the present owner. The quilt was made in 1868 when Dora Stevens was twenty-one years old and it might have been part of her trousseau, for she married George H. Rush on November 24, 1869.

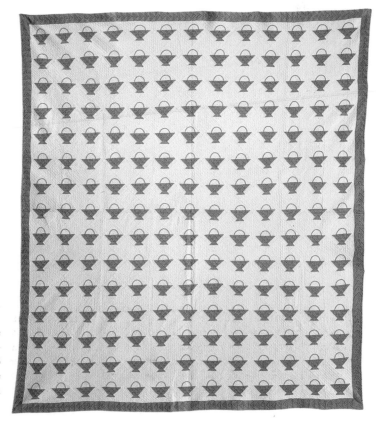

156. Flower Basket; made by Mary Jane Mead (1830–1896); Quaker Street, Schenectady County; 1840s; pieced and appliquéd cotton with stuffed work; 81″ x 75″. (Collection of Miss Dorothy Mead) This basket quilt differs from others of the type because every basket carries a different flower or fruit. Of particular interest is the weeping willow in one basket; it is possible that this was intended as a memorial block, but no information is available to confirm or deny this. All the flowers in the border as well as those in the baskets are made with stuffed work. Mary Jane Mead was born in Quaker Street of Quaker parents. The maker was the grandmother of the present owner.

most important one, the scrap basket, in which treasures are stored until they are taken to form a careful part of another quilt.[4]

Whatever their original source, Basket designs occur over and over and lend themselves well to individual interpretation. Many of the Basket quilts seen showed an imaginative bent—and sometimes tongue-in-cheek humor—in what the quiltmakers chose to put in their baskets. A particularly pleasing version is the quilt made by Mary Jane Mead, which has every basket filled with a different object, including a weeping willow tree.

Irish Chain, of which single, double, and triple variations were seen, was first recorded in the mid nineteenth century. It is possible that it is actually based on a weaving draft—there are both Overshot and Double Weave designs to which this pattern bears a remarkable similarity—and may date from as early as 1800.

Fan patterns are noted in an 1885 issue of *Peterson's Magazine* as being entirely new, and Barbara Brackman gives them a date of about 1880.[5] The favorite Dresden

Plate may be seen as a variation on the Fan pattern, as it did not become common until a number of years later.

Log Cabin, another favorite pattern with many distinct variations, is a bit more problematical as to its origin. Although some have dated it from just after the Civil War,[6] others are of the opinion that it is time for a revision in thought. According to this scenario, Log Cabin was a type of quilt that originated in Great Britain—Scotland seems to be the most-mentioned probable source—several hundred years ago and was embraced by quilters here in the nineteenth century.[7] While there seems to be evidence to substantiate this hypothesis, one may still question why a centuries-old British pattern that was not particularly obscure did not appear here before the mid nineteenth century when emigrants must certainly have brought knowledge of it with them at an earlier date. Again, an intriguing mystery with the final answer yet to be found.

In Log Cabin patterns, the organization of blocks can form either a single large and dramatic design when sewn

157. Chain; maker unknown; New York; first quarter nineteenth century; cotton with stuffed work; 84″ x 72″. (Collection of Oysterponds Historical Society, Inc., Orient, Long Island; Gift of Isabelle Knobloch) Although the red fabric that makes up the chain pattern is in very fragile condition, this quilt is a splendid example of pieced and stuffed work with exquisite quilting. The monogram "MTV" is worked in stuffed work in the center row of diamonds, and the knitted fringe is handsome and original. The Oysterponds Historical Society states that the quilt was said to be "over 100 years old" when it was given to the society in 1956, but nothing is known about this expert quiltmaker.

158. Triple Irish Chain; made by Ann Van Nest Bussing (1811–1905); New York City; 1833–1835; pieced cotton; 98″ x 98″. (Collection of Museum of the City of New York, 34.90.43; Gift of Miss Mary Bussing) Unlike most chain patterns, which often seem to have more consistent palettes, this Irish Chain uses a wide range of fabrics. The variety shown here serves as a good guide to the many contemporary prints to which Ann Van Nest Bussing had access. The quiltmaker was the sixth child of Margaret Field and Abraham Van Nest, a civic-minded dry-goods merchant active in Reformed Church affairs, who also served as a New York City alderman in 1833. Ann Van Nest married John Schermerhorn Bussing on August 23, 1833, and she probably made this quilt early in her married life.

159. Log Cabin—unique design; maker unknown; Hornby area, Steuben County; date unknown; pieced cotton, wool, and serge; 81″ x 72″. (Collection of Rheon Williams) This quilt is an outstanding example of originality at work in the Log Cabin style, for the artist produced one of the most powerful and exciting Log Cabin designs we have ever seen. The background blocks are pieced from scrap fabrics, but the swirling design in red and blue was most likely created from fabric specially purchased or set aside for this purpose. The only information the present owner has about this quilt is that it was passed down from her mother; she does know that neither her mother nor her grandmother made it.

160. Log Cabin—variation of Barn Raising design; maker unknown; Rochester, Monroe County; 1900–1910; cotton and rayon; 76″ x 76″. (Collection of Ione Collins) The present owner purchased this dramatic example of a Log Cabin quilt at the Seton Shop of St. Mary's Hospital in Rochester, New York. The fabrics used in this quilt appear to be scraps of material used for men's vests and suits.

161. Log Cabin—Pineapple design; made by Cornelia Van Wyck (1839–1912); Dutchess County; c. 1875; pieced silk; 68″ x 48″. (Private collection) Although this quilt was purchased at an antiques shop, it had been documented prior to its sale and more research on the part of the present owner verifies that it was made by Cornelia Van Wyck when she was in her mid-thirties. She used satin fabrics from a top-hat factory in Dutchess County and made a quilt for each of her daughters, Antoinette, Harriet, and Elizabeth. One of the quilts is on display at the Van Wyck Museum in Fishkill, New York, one has not been located and is presumed to be lost or no longer in existence, and this one is the third. The Van Wycks were an early family in the Hudson Valley and were members of the Dutch Reformed Church. The quilt formerly belonged to a great-granddaughter of the maker.

162. Cornelia Van Wyck

together or a series of smaller ones. Fabrics were usually carefully chosen to emphasize the contrasts required to carry out the overall design. Log Cabin patterns derive from the appearance of the overall pattern and include such a wide variety as Barn Raising, Windmill Blades, Light and Dark, Courthouse Steps, Pineapple, and Streak o' Lightning. All these variations and more were seen during the Project, and the creative range available through the variation of color and shade alone was quite astonishing and gave some sense of the scope of artistic expression that women exhibited through this homely medium.

Album quilts in all their many forms were often among the most carefully preserved of the quilts documented, presenting clear testimonials to the position and value of the receiver to her or his community. By the late 1820s, it was fashionable for books known as "annuals" (also advertised as "albums") to be sold, particularly as New Year's presents. Relatives and friends could write poems, good wishes, or appropriate quotations in the book and embellish the pages with drawings and elaborate calligraphy. It is possible that these annual autograph or album books, as they came to be known, were the design sources for the writings on many of the friendship or signature quilts that were so popular starting just before the mid nineteenth century.[8] "An album quilt is a very pretty idea," notes a popular book of the time. "A lady gives the size of the square she wishes to each of her lady friends who are willing to contribute to her quilt. They make a square according to their own taste, putting a white piece in the

center on which they write their name. Every lady's autograph adorns her own square."[9] As the nation became more and more mobile and people left their close-knit home communities for the prospective advantages offered by new jobs or land availability elsewhere, ties to those left behind took on major importance, and a signed quilt, a tangible sign of caring and remembrance, could offer comfort when the physical presence could not be had. Sometimes these quilts simply signaled a change in the status of the person gifted, as in the case of a quilt made for a trousseau or wedding or for retirement, but most often, whatever the text actually inscribed on them, they carried the heartfelt message "remember me."

Numerous red, green, and white quilts were seen in the course of the Project; they were particularly notable for the range of design variation that occurred within a limited number of recurring patterns—namely, Whig Rose, Rose of Sharon, Rose Wreath, and Cockscomb. Although the initial impression when looking at many of these quilts together is one of identical design within the pattern blocks, a closer look usually reflects significant differences, such as in the materials chosen, a subtle addition of another color, and in the basic design itself—and especially in the border designs and quilting patterns. There is no absolute answer as to why these quilts were so popular from about the 1830s through 1900. Brackman speculates that, as the patterns themselves are imitations of nature, the colors too are meant to reflect the real-life reds and greens of flowers and leaves.[10] The colors themselves also make a strong statement against the stark background whites, and this contrast as much as anything may have contributed to their popularity. The fabrics used were rarely pure reds or greens—they were almost invariably cut from small-scale calicos and there is a tremendous amount of variation in the fabric patterns seen.

Red, green, and white designs are frequently associated with the more decorative patterns and more elaborate quilting, thus giving rise to the speculation that these were not everyday quilts but usually meant for a special occasion. In many cases, this combination is known to have been used for trousseau or wedding-gift quilts, which gives some credence to this belief, but others may have been made simply because the maker liked the idea or found the style well-suited to show off her skills.

Another common color combination seen was deep blue and white—again, the blues were rarely solid but more likely to be a background for tiny white, yellow, or multicolored figures. These quilts could be pieced or appliqué or even a combination of techniques, and the most prevalent patterns for this type of quilt were Feathered Stars or designs that appear to be based on papercuts and often show great originality. Another common feature of these quilts is a repetitive tree border, although this border is not, by any means, generic to all

163. Album; made by a member of the Snook family; Fishkill, Dutchess County; 1860; appliquéd cotton; 91″ x 77″. (Collection of Fishkill Historical Society, Fishkill, N.Y.) Of the thirty blocks in this album quilt, eleven have inscriptions and one is dated 1860. Some of the inscriptions merely state "Cousin Julia," "Cousin Emily," "Debbie L," or "Mary," but research shows that the quilt descended in the Snook family and is considered a family Album. The researcher used family genealogies derived from family bibles to track some names, and a direct relationship to the donor of the quilt to the historical society—the granddaughter of Gilbert and Antoinette Snook—can be shown.

164. Mexican Rose variation; made by or for Sarah Williams; Berkshire, Tioga County; 1830; appliquéd cotton; 101″ x 70″. (Collection of Ethel Curkendall) The family history is unclear as to whether this quilt was made for Sarah Williams at her birth (1830) or for her later engagement. The red, green, and white palette and controlled floral design could conceivably place the quilt more toward mid-century or later rather than 1830. Sarah Williams's family were beekeepers.

SARAH.B.BO.1830.SARAH.WILLIAMS.

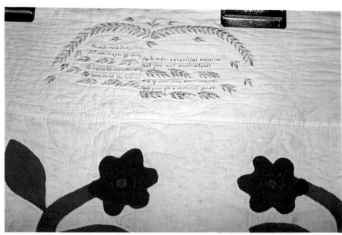

165 and 165a. Flower of Paradise (Whig Rose); made by Mrs. R. Page; Carroll, Chautauqua County; March 28, 1862; appliquéd cotton; 82″ x 80″. (Collection of Doris A. Holt) Although the basic pattern for this quilt is Whig Rose, it has been titled Flower of Paradise because of the three India ink cartouches along the top border. The center and most elaborate one contains the words "Flower of Paradise." The cartouche at the right contains the maker's name, the place where it was made, and the date. The cartouche at the left contains the following poem: "There blooms a lovely flower;/ It blooms in a far off land;/ Its life has a beautiful mission/ That few will understand;/ Its leaves illumine the valley;/ Its odors scent the wood;/ And if evil ones come near it;/ They grow in a moment good!" The present owner is the great-great-granddaughter of the maker.

166. Oak Leaf and Acorn; made by Emily Holbert (b. 1820); Chester, Orange County; 1847; appliquéd cotton; 102″ x 85″. (Collection of Smithsonian Institution, Washington, D.C.; Gift of Mr. and Mrs. John Beard Ecker) Emily Holbert, daughter of James and Susan Drake Holbert of Chester, added a strong sentiment to her lovely interpretation of this classic red, green, and white quilt when she appliquéd not only her name, the date, and location on it but also "Industry, and Proper Improvement of Time. 1847 Vanity of Vanities, All Is Vanity." Mrs. Ecker is the great-niece of the maker.

167. Tulip variation; made by Ann Elizabeth Vanderlyn (1835–1926); Montgomery, Orange County; 1855; appliquéd cotton; 93″ x 76″. (Collection of Mary Vanderlyn Hazen) Ann Elizabeth Vanderlyn made this quilt at the age of twenty, a year before her marriage. It is presumed that the quilt was part of the contents of her hope chest. A story that has been passed down in the family is that some of her friends offered to help by making one of the blocks in the quilt, but the donated block didn't meet her standards, so Ann Elizabeth tore it out and did it over herself. Ann Elizabeth grew up in New Paltz, Ulster County, and married Robert Sinsabaugh, a fruit and dairy farmer from the Montgomery area, in 1856. They had six children, five of whom lived into adulthood. The Vanderlyn family is Dutch, and their presence in America dates back to the earliest days of New Amsterdam. Ann Elizabeth was a direct descendant of Pieter Vanderlyn, one of the most important of the eighteenth-century patroon painters of the Hudson Valley.

168. Ann Elizabeth Vanderlyn

blue and white quilts in New York State. The quilting in these is often quite spectacular, and this, plus the care that seems to be taken generally in the piecing and appliqué work, would indicate that such quilts may have been intended as "best" quilts by the makers. Brackman uses the early 1830s as the beginning point for similar quilts, and notes that the blue and white woven coverlets of earlier years may have served as inspiration for them.[11]

From the sample of quilts registered, the Princess Feather, although a favorite design for quilting, did not seem to have the same popularity as an appliqué pattern in New York as it did in other parts of the country after about 1850. The design itself is thought to be of earlier origin; one attribution ties it to the coat of arms of the original Prince of Wales, Edward II, in 1307; it is believed to have developed in Northumberland and Durham, where variations occurred over the generations, including the gender change from "prince's" to "princess."[12] Corroboration of the design may be seen in two portraits. One is of Edward VI as a child painted by Hans Holbein the Younger (1497–1543), which shows Edward wearing an elaborate headdress with an ostrich-type plume. The second portrait is of Henry, Prince of Wales, circa 1610, painted by Robert Peake, in which the prince is seen

169. Feathered Star; made by Elizabeth Taylor Onderdonk Mead (1832–1921); Selkirk, Albany County; before 1900; pieced cotton; 86″ x 76″. Photograph by Fred Ricard. (Collection of Mary Lou Bulnes) Documentation shows that Elizabeth Mead was born in Niskayuna, Albany County, and was married to David Mead. She made this quilt from scraps of dressmaking fabrics and was probably helped by at least one of her sisters. The present owner is the great-granddaughter of the maker.

170. Blazing Star; piecing and appliqué work by Sarah Permelia Peck (b. 1814), quilting by the Roses Brook Methodist Church Ladies Missionary Group; Stamford, Delaware County; 1845; pieced and appliquéd cotton with reverse appliqué and stuffed work; 85″ x 85″. (Collection of Janice Rich-Russomando) This Blazing Star is in the indigo blue and white palette so favored in this part of the state at mid nineteenth century. The piecing and appliqué work on the quilt is exquisitely precise, and it is said that the maker of the top, Sarah Permelia Peck, was most unhappy with the quality of the quilting done by the Ladies Missionary Group. She thought that the stitches (eight to the inch) were much too large to complement her careful work on the top! Only two sides of the quilt have the birds-on-a-bough pattern above the border, and the present owner likes to speculate that perhaps the bed for which it was intended was kept against a wall, thus keeping one side of the quilt from showing.

171. Princess Feather; made by Sarah Milks Cummings (1828–1881); Onondaga County; 1850; appliquéd cotton with stuffed work; 80″ x 78″. (Collection of Mrs. Jane Cummings Amidon) Sarah Milks Cummings, born in the town of Navarino in Onondaga County, made this quilt when she was twenty-two years old. She has turned the basic Princess Feather pattern into a truly original design concept with the inclusion of cherry trees and birds feeding on cherries. Although the appliqué work has been extensively—and not always expertly—repaired, the beautiful original quilting remains. This quilt was the inspiration for a folk art painting, *Cherry Tree*, by Ruth Reed Cummings, the mother of the present owner and a direct descendant of the quiltmaker, whose paintings of life in central New York at the turn of the century evoke poignant memories for local residents.

wearing a headdress with a triple plume symbolic of Wales. Another theory as to its origin refers to the plumes worn by English knights and ladies.[13]

Stenciled spreads were somewhat rare. The few that were seen were unquilted, and they were probably made for decorative purposes rather than everyday use because the fine cotton or linen that usually serves as a base for this type of quilt would most likely not hold up as well as the heavier stitched quilts. The dates of stenciled spreads seem to coincide with the fad for theorem painting and the popular decorative technique of stenciled designs on walls, furniture, and floors. The designs, for the most part, reflected stylized flowers, fruit, trees, birds, and other naturalistic motifs. Stenciling lent itself well to tinware, and Ann Butler, maker of the quilt shown on page 66, helped her father, well-known tinsmith Aaron Butler, with such decoration.

Stenciling was not difficult to do, requiring only time and a reasonably steady hand. Patterns would be cut out of oiled paper and then laid on a well-anchored foundation fabric. A different stencil is used for each color. Color was prepared in two ways: a concentrated dye could be mixed with gum arabic, which would not run under the stencil and blur the edges, but it would fade quickly. The more common way was to use a ground pigment in oil with a stencil mordant that set the colors more permanently. (Keep in mind that these were all natural pigments, aniline dyes not being available until after the mid-1800s.) The paint was tamped with balls of cotton held in shape with a coarse cotton cover through the stencil opening, one color at a time, with drying time allowed between colors. Colors were sometimes shaded to give a sense of dimensionality.[14]

Pieced lettering seemed to be a typical New York convention (although not limited to New York) and quite possibly grew out of the sampler-making tradition for young girls, as many of these quilts bore a distinct resemblance in style of lettering and composition to these earlier needlework efforts. Quilts using pieced lettering and bearing the greatest similarities to sampler techniques

172. Stenciled coverlet; maker unknown; Ulster County; c. 1830; pieced cotton; 92″ x 82″. (Collection of Susan Parrish Antiques, New York City) This quilt was probably made only for decorative use, for the fine cotton fabric would not stand up to everyday wear. Stenciled spreads are somewhat rare; they are usually unquilted like this one, and the stenciled border seems to indicate that it was intended to be used just as a summer spread.

173. Monogram Medallion; made by a member of the DuBois family; New Paltz, Ulster County; 1807; pieced cotton; 86″ x 72″. (Courtesy America Hurrah Antiques, New York City) This quilt, using pieced lettering in a Central Medallion design, comes from New Paltz; it was purchased in a DuBois family estate sale and is thought to have been made by an early member of the family, which has lived in the area for many years. It bears a striking similarity to another quilt documented in Ulster County and dated 1811, which suggests the possibility that this type of quilt with the pieced initials or name and date in the center was a design convention of the region during that period of time.

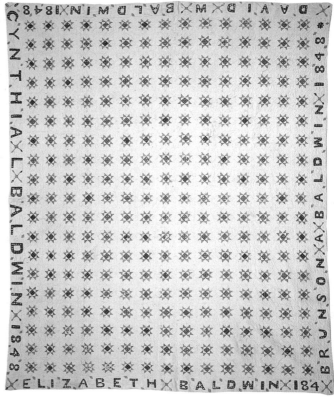

174. Evening Star; probably made by a member of the Baldwin family; Duanesburg, Schenectady County; 1848; pieced cotton; 92¼″ x 76¾. (Collection of New York State Museum, Albany, N.Y.) Elizabeth, Brunson A., David W., and Cynthia L. Baldwin all have their names appliquéd on this interesting quilt, but we do not know why the quilt was made. The date is appliquéd after each name, only the second "8" on the date after Elizabeth's name was left out—poor space planning on the part of the quiltmaker!

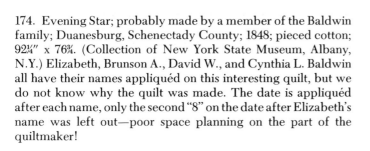

175. Lady of the Lake variation; made by Mary H. Luce Terry (1837–1925); Riverhead, Suffolk County; 1890; pieced cotton; 92½″ x 77″. (Collection of Hallockville Incorporated) Mary Luce Terry, married to Daniel S. Terry, lived all her life in the township of Riverhead in Suffolk County. She was a member of the Congregational Church on Sound Avenue, which had a very active and well-known quilt group called the Sound Avenue Ladies. She used both traditional and popular sources for her quilt designs. A young friend, who was quoted in *Sound Avenue Ladies*, p. 17, remembered her as always wearing "long black dresses or a black skirt. She was hemming most of the time I saw her—[she] used to make hand towels out of sugar sacks. I remember seeing her pull the string out and then she'd pin a piece of that material to her long skirt and then she'd just hem up all the way. It fascinated me as a youngster. And I loved to hem after that."

176. Mary H. Luce Terry

for the most part predated 1850; those of the latter part of the century tended to use the lettering more as a decorative element in borders or as a convention for signing a name rather than as the major compositional element of the design. Appliquéd lettering became much more common than pieced after the mid-century.

The Lady of the Lake pattern was seen quite often in all regions during the Quilt Days. The pattern name begins to be associated with a variation of a sawtooth pattern soon after the publication of Sir Walter Scott's poem of the same name. This poem of the manners and customs of the picturesque Scottish highlands and lakes seems to have appealed to the romanticism of the young women of the nineteenth century, and it was a favorite bit of literature both at school and at home. Why this particular pattern was associated with the poem is not known, although the jagged points and alternating blank areas may have represented to those who first attached the name to the pattern the jutting tors, windswept moors, and shimmering waters of Scott's beloved highlands.

Delectable Mountains is another favorite pattern with several distinct variations and thought to be an old one. It is only one of many pattern names inspired by religious verses or text.[15] The name is derived from John Bunyan's allegory, *Pilgrim's Progress*, written in 1675 while the author was imprisoned for his religious beliefs. The

pilgrims in the tale, after a journey of great travail, eventually come upon the Delectable Mountains:

> …and behold at a great distance he saw a most pleasant
> Mountainous Country, Beautiful with Woods, Vineyards,
> Fruits and all sorts, Flowers also, and with Springs and
> Fountains, very delectable to behold…. They went
> till they came to the Delectable Mountains….
> And when thou comest There from thence, said they,
> thou mayest see to the gate of the Celestial City.

All the Delectable Mountains patterns seen had exquisite needlework and fabrics that appeared to have been bought or collected specifically for the quilt. Perhaps the concept alone provided a spur to the quilters to do their best for the pattern!

Mariner's Compass, another favorite pattern but one that required considerable skill to do properly, has sixteen to thirty-two points arranged in a circle, with four being more prominent than others. It is thought to have been

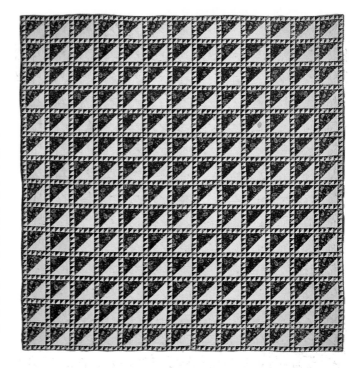

177. Sawtooth (Lady of the Lake); probably made by Susannah Yerkes Bliss; New York; 1835–1850; pieced cotton; 94½″ x 90″. Photograph by Mark Gulezian. (Collection of DAR Museum, Washington, D.C.; Gift of Miss Marjorie Strang) Family history attributes this quilt to having been part of the trousseau of Susannah Yerkes Bliss and put its date at about 1811. However, the textiles, which include a discharge-printed brown print and a roller-printed blue print, as well as the style of the quilt make it far more probable that it was made between 1835 and 1850. Susannah was alive during this period and could still have been its maker.

178. Delectable Mountains variation; made by Cornelia H. Smith; Monroe, Orange County; August 4, 1847; cotton; 91″ x 71″. (Collection of Nancy Scrivner) This quilt was purchased almost by accident in April 1974 at an outdoor estate auction in Monroe. The weather was rainy, misty, cool, and generally uncomfortable for an outdoor auction. The auctioneer had a number of quilts to sell, none of which was opened. The present owner and her husband bought the quilt mainly to provide themselves with some protection from the uncomfortable weather. They did not discover until after they had purchased it that it was signed and dated "Cornelia H. Smith, Monroe, NY, August 4, 1847." The quilt has a beard guard (the white overlay fabric at the top), and both the white pieced cross at the center of the quilt and the cross-in-a-circle quilting set this off from standard interpretations of the Delectable Mountains pattern.

179. Delectable Mountains or Sawtooth variation; maker unknown; upstate New York, near Watertown; c. 1845; pieced cotton; 90″ x 76″. (Courtesy Laura Fisher/Antique Quilts & Americana, New York City) A fragment of paper attached to the quilt carried the name Susan, but whether this referred to the quiltmaker or an owner is unclear. The pattern is an unusual variation on the traditional Delectable Mountains, and the wide border, with its several exquisitely executed quilting designs, adds much to the graphic quality of the quilt. The quiltmaker has used her limited amount of red fabric judiciously and created a sense of movement in the design by its skillful placement.

inspired by the compass designs on sea charts of the seventeenth through nineteenth centuries, with the four more prominent points representing the compass directionals north, south, east, and west. There are quilt patterns identical or similar to Mariner's Compass but called by other names, such as Rising Sun, Sunburst, Rising Star.[16] The name differences could have to do with geography; a quilter in a coastal area where ships are a way of life might be more likely to use the name Mariner's Compass, while landbound quilters might relate more easily to one of the other names. Mariner's Compass quilts may be pieced or appliqué, and both types were seen.

Whole Cloth is a category rather than a pattern and covers a multitude of fabrics and types of worked spreads, a large number of which were also documented. Whole-cloth spreads were made of several long strips of one fabric sewn together to form a textile wide enough to cover a bed, and these were then stenciled or embroidered, then batted, backed, and quilted. Many, but not all, of these were whitework. According to Jean Taylor Federico, "There are three major types of white work bedcovering; embroidery, candlewicking, and Marseilles quilting or stuffed work."[17] The simple white ground fabric, usually linen or cotton, provided an effective backdrop for the decorative stitching that usually covered the spread. Often these pieces feature names, dates, and locations of the makers or recipients in addition to the

spectacular quilted and stuffed patterns that formed flowers, baskets, fruits, feathered borders, and sometimes even animals. Of interest is that this type of stuffed work has usually been referred to by today's quiltmakers as "trapunto," a term that never appeared in nineteenth-century inventories. Only one example of "zaam stickewerke," an especially elaborate form of quilting and stuffed work topped with embroidery that has roots in Holland, was located (see page 9), and, appropriately enough, it was made by a quilter of Dutch lineage.

A few examples of roller-printed whole-cloth quilts were seen, but the majority of the remainder were of calimanco, sometimes erroneously called linsey-woolsey.[18] This heavy fabric was made of wool and finished with a highly glazed luster that served admirably as a ground for decorative quilting and stuffed work. Calimancos were commonly dyed a range of brilliant colors with natural dyes, and several examples in a rich green-blue (one said to be dyed with walnut hulls) were seen, along with some in raspberry red, light blue, and green. Calimancos had almost disappeared from popular use by about 1825, as the range of fabrics—particularly prints—available for general purchase had increased substantially by that time and women began to look for variety rather than the subtleties offered by whole-cloth work.

Trees turned up with great regularity as a motif in New

180. Mariner's Compass; made by Emeline Barker (1820–1906); New York City; date unknown; pieced and appliquéd cotton; 98″ x 98″. (Collection of Museum of the City of New York, 44.31.8; Gift of Mrs. Marian Place Hildrith) This is probably the finest Mariner's Compass quilt seen by the Quilt Project. Each thin radiating spike comes to a perfect point, and the stitches throughout are tiny and exquisitely placed. It was made by Emeline Barker, who lived with her sister on 26th Street in New York City. The quilt is signed "Emeline Barker #7."

181. Mariner's Compass; thought to have been made by Margaret Charlesworth (1826–1906); Avoca; Steuben County; mid nineteenth century; pieced and appliquéd cotton; 97″ x 80″. (Collection of Jeanne Townsend) The present owner notes that this quilt was given to her father as a bequest from the estate of neighbors, Mr. and Mrs. John Charlesworth. As a child, he had been very close to this family, and in a letter written to his daughter in 1972, he recalled this special friendship: "When I was a boy growing up, I called Mrs. C. 'Grandma' and Mr. C. 'Pa Charlesworth'. I spent a lot of my time at their house, & ate many meals there. I remember Grandma as a great cook.... Grandma used to hang this quilt, & other things out for airing once a year. Thats [sic] the only time I'd see it."

182. Whole Cloth; made by Chloe Jane Filkens (1853–1926); Sodus, Wayne County; 1871; white cotton with stuffed work; 89″ x 75″. (Collection of Florence Merritt) This quilt was purchased at an auction at the home of Dr. and Mrs. Morris Beal of Sodus, New York, in 1976, and Dr. Beal, the step-grandson of the quiltmaker, provided the present owner with whatever information he had. Chloe Jane Filkens, the maker, would have been eighteen years old when she made the quilt in 1871, and it is possible that she made it for her hope chest. Despite the quilt being in the bridal tradition, Chloe did not marry until March 27, 1890, at which time she married her cousin's widower, Washington Irving Waterbury, and brought up his two small daughters in their home three miles south of Sodus.

183. Tree of Life; maker unknown; Ulster County; mid nineteenth century; appliquéd and embroidered cotton; 99½" x 80⅜". (Collection of Smithsonian Institution, Washington, D.C.) This counterpane was made for Dr. Josiah Hasbrouck and his wife, Ellen Jane Blauvelt. Dr. Hasbrouck was a medical doctor, and the quilt was possibly made for him by a grateful patient, or, perhaps, in recognition of his service to his community. The lady and gentleman under the tree are said to be the Hasbroucks, and the four boys in rowboats are presumably their sons. Most intriguing are the letters of the alphabet that are appliquéd randomly over the counterpane; the alphabet is incomplete, yet some letters are used more than once.

The piece is a primer of fabrics covering a fifty-year span. The earliest is a block print that may date from the 1790s; others are block- and roller-printed cottons, some glazed, ranging from about 1800 to 1840–1845. Some of the later fabrics have stippled shading with blue added by surface roller. On the reverse side of one panel of the white ground is stamped "Fine Sheeting," the number "31" in a wreath of leaves, and a vase of flowers on a platform.

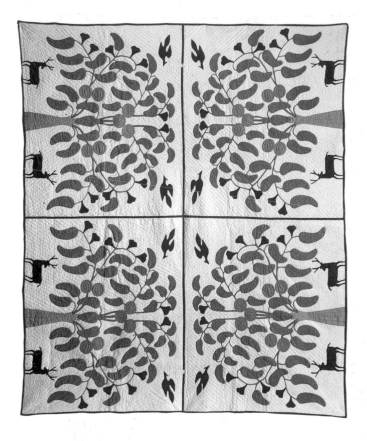

184. Tree of Life; maker unknown; probably Andes, Delaware County; 1860s; appliquéd cotton; 90″ x 74½″. (Collection of Helen M. Kie) This unusual version of a Tree of Life quilt is a good example of how a treasured heirloom will remain in a family through the years. Although the maker is not known, it *is* known that Mary Calhoun gave the quilt to her daughter, Mary Elizabeth Calhoun (1874–1962), and it remained with her in Andes until 1911, when Mary Elizabeth moved to West Newark, Tioga County, to become the second wife of Wallace Hover. Wallace and Mary Elizabeth had no children, but he had a daughter by his first marriage, Mary Louise Hover. In October 1926, Wallace and Mary Elizabeth moved back to Andes after the sale of the family homestead to Mary Elizabeth's nephews, taking the quilt with them. Wallace died in Andes in 1938, but was buried in West Newark. Apparently the quilt was then given to Mary Louise, who later gave it to her son and daughter-in-law, Raymond and Helen Kie, who still own it today.

York quilts. Some assumed naturalistic forms and served as the focal point of the quilt while others formed elegant stylized borders. Weeping willows were a running theme, especially in the lovely blue and white quilts that seemed to predominate from Columbia and Dutchess Counties in the eastern part of the state across the Hudson River into Ulster and Delaware Counties. Many of these quilts with tree borders also had birds appliquéd onto the trees. Whether the weeping willow carried its usual symbolism relating to death and mourning in these cases is not known; in any case, the weeping willow has a strong graphic quality and was most likely used as a design element for this reason alone.

The pine tree, another element laden with symbolism, also appeared frequently in quilt designs either in a stylized or more abstract form. A significant symbol since ancient times, the pine tree has been used by many cultures to denote spiritual values, redemption, and immortality,[19] and it was included in the mourning pictures stitched by schoolgirls earlier in the century as a symbol of everlasting life. Suellen Meyer theorizes in an article about Pine Tree quilts that from the very earliest days of settlement on the American continent the pine tree, because of its abundance and usefulness, played an important role in the life of the settler, thus making it natural that it would be immortalized as a quilt pattern.[20] The pine tree also had secular symbolism to Americans; it was the symbol on the first coins minted in 1652 in the Massachusetts Bay Colony, and it was the insignia flown by the first war vessels of the new nation. Meyer also notes that throughout most of the nineteenth century, the Pine Tree pattern name and design remained the same, but when variations began to occur late in the century, a simultaneous variation in name also occurred. It was sometimes called Tree of Life.

Crazy quilts—which are rarely quilts in the true sense, as they are generally tied, or "tufted" rather than quilted— were a rampant fad everywhere in the country from the late 1870s through the turn of the century, and New York was no exception. The term *Crazy* describes the random, irregular fabric scraps and patterns used to compose these eccentric creations, which allowed every maker's imagination to run riot in the combination of colors, fabrics, and decorative techniques used. There are several theories as to the origin of the term, the most popular being purely descriptive of a work that has no seeming rhyme or reason.[21] The Crazy style was first known as "Japanese patchwork," and Penny McMorris notes that the inspiration for Crazy quilts probably had its roots in the Philadelphia Centennial Exposition of 1876, at which Japanese decorative arts were seen for the first time in the United States: "Some of the screens exhibited there were described as being covered with textured gilt paper ornamented with patches of various materials that had

185. Snowflake with Tree Border; made by M. R. Henderson (1848–1918); Margaretville, Delaware County; c. 1850; appliquéd cotton; 92″ x 72″. (Collection of Eleanor Faulkner) The present owner, who received the quilt through her husband, knows only that the name of the maker was "Aunt Net Henderson." It is inscribed "M.R. Henderson" in one of the corners. The "weeping" tree border used on this quilt relates it to other similar borders that seem to be endemic to the quilts of New York State; the dramatic use of blue and white in a bold and repetitive cut-out pattern also is common to many of the quilts found from the Hudson Valley area west to the Catskills.

186. Tree of Life (Pine Tree variation); made by Julia Marie Blackney Hall; Perrysburg, Cattaraugus County; second half nineteenth century; pieced cotton; 92″ x 90″. (Collection of Kecia Binko) This quilt was made by the great-great-grandmother of the present owner. It is known that the quiltmaker, Julia M. Blackney of Perrysburg, Cattaraugus County, married John E. Hall on April 4, 1876, but virtually nothing else is known about her life. There is no certainty as to the date it was made, but style and fabrics would place it as about 1860 or later. Also, although the pine tree is a frequently appearing motif in quilts, this rather stylized repetitive placement with extensive sashing was not typically seen until the mid to late nineteenth century.

187. Marriage certificate of Julia M. Blackney and John E. Hall

188. Detail of Rising Star variation; made by Elsey A. Halstead (1830–1850); Minisink (now Middletown), Orange County; 1848; pieced and appliquéd cotton. The complete quilt is illustrated on page 102. (Collection of Margaret Halstead Minch)

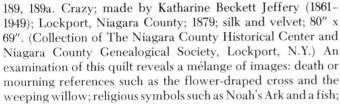

189, 189a. Crazy; made by Katharine Beckett Jeffery (1861–1949); Lockport, Niagara County; 1879; silk and velvet; 80″ x 69″. (Collection of The Niagara County Historical Center and Niagara County Genealogical Society, Lockport, N.Y.) An examination of this quilt reveals a mélange of images: death or mourning references such as the flower-draped cross and the weeping willow; religious symbols such as Noah's Ark and a fish; and the more popular Crazy quilt patterns, such as the animal appliqués and the heavily embroidered figures. The maker was born and raised in Geneva, New York, and later married Daniel Elwood Jeffery. When she died in 1949 at the age of 89, the quilt was donated to the Niagara Historical Society by two granddaughters living in Michigan.

painted, embroidered, or quilted designs."[22] And commenting on the rage for Oriental styles, a weekly home-decorating column noted that, "It is the novelty that makes Chinese and Japanese goods so popular with us and Europeans; in form, construction, ornamentation and decoration, the products of the Japanese differ from anything produced elsewhere."[23] The sheer numbers indicate the popularity of the Crazy style, but perhaps it was more than a simple fad and satisfied a certain need of even the most prosaic needlewoman, as explained in the words of an anonymous woman, who said: "I think it is a pleasant variety after the coarser work and unending array of plain sewing which is always confronting the housekeeper, to take up the soft materials whose bright colors refresh the eyes, and form them into tasteful ornaments for the home."[24]

The Crazy quilt fad did not meet with the unanimous approval of the nation, and numerous articles and letters appeared in the popular magazines of the times taking women to task for what was, to some, a prodigious waste of talent, time, and effort. In 1884, at the height of the Crazy craze, *Harper's Bazar* published a rather scathing commentary on the phenomenon:

We were asked to join in a raffle for a crazy quilt made up of 9,000 scraps of silk and satin set together with much ingenuity of design and niceness of stitching. To the maker and her friends it appeared a monumental labor of taste, industry and artistic talent. To us it stood for misdirected energy and perseverance too common among women. If it cost but 10 minutes to add one scrap to another—an allowance far too small—the quilt represented an outlay of 1,500 hours, 123 working days of 12 solid hours each or one hour a day for more than 4 years.

What might not this industrious young woman have accomplished in that time? If she really cared for decorative art 1,500 hours of close study and practice would have developed an admirable and remunerative skill in embroi-

190. Sampler Crazy; made by Catherine (1796–1886), Sarah Brinckerhoff (1794–1878), and Wilhelmina Maria (1793–1873) Van Wagenen; Oxford, Chenango County; third quarter nineteenth century; pieced silk; 68″ x 64″. (Collection of Barbara Parker Chasis) The three sisters who are said to have made this quilt were in their twenties when their family moved from New York City to Oxford in 1820. They never married, and they lived together in the house in Oxford until their deaths. They were great-great-aunts to the present owner, who found the quilt in her grandmother's house in Oxford after her death. The owner of this most unusual quilt notes that she always had the impression from her grandfather's diary that the sisters were not happy to be uprooted from the activities that had kept them busy in New York City.

dery and painting. They would have sufficed for the acquisition of a modern language, a sound knowledge of history, poetry, literature, art, music. They might have been exchanged for the important science of housekeeping and kitchen chemistry.

The craze for decorative art has wrought certain definite mischiefs without much good.... The cumulative teaching of all time having been that women should be satisfied with patchwork, mental, moral and manual, it is perhaps unreasonable to expect them to repudiate it....[25]

Although one publication prematurely noted the death of the Crazy quilt, it accurately reported the next rage: "The Japanese crazy quilt has been finally laid to rest; but its speedy successor, the brilliantly colored ribbon quilt, has a legion of admirers; these spreads are easily made; the principal requirement is a slight knowledge of the mingling of colors; the ribbons chosen are very narrow, about half an inch in width and of all colors; they are woven together in basket fashion, when the desired width is obtained a border is added of ribbon about three or four inches in width and finished at the edges with soft lace."[26]

In spite of this enthusiasm, only a few ribbon quilts

192. Crazy with Tumbling Blocks; made by Martha M. Giffin (1815–1896); New York City; 1886; silk and velvet; 67″ x 56″. (Collection of Margaret Giffin Siegel) This brilliant silk and velvet quilt uses Tumbling Blocks as the basis for its design. It carries the inscription "Mary from M.A. 1886" and was made by Martha Giffin for her daughter. The quiltmaker was born in Northeast, Dutchess County; she lived at 19 Bank Street in New York City and was seventy-one years old when the quilt was made. She was the great-grandmother of the present owner.

193. For making Crazy quilts, women could order scrap silks, embroidery-stamping outfits, and ready-to-sew-on appliqués from catalogues. Page from the *Ladies' Art Co.* catalog. (Courtesy Phyllis A. Tepper)

194. Penny Squares; made by Helen Ulrich Taylor (b. 1912); Buffalo, Erie County; late 1930s; pieced cotton; 91″ x 80½″. (Collection of Jeanne Hegedus-Leary) Helen Ulrich Taylor, the quiltmaker, was born in South Buffalo. She took up sewing in the eighth grade and later learned to quilt with a group of ladies at the Salem Lutheran Church. Unlike many people who made Penny Squares, Helen Taylor made her own designs, often tracing them out of a children's coloring book rather than buying preprinted patterns. (One square has a bat and ball on it because her husband was a baseball player.) She used red and white in the quilt because it was very fashionable at the time, but she never used the quilt because she did not have a red bedroom. When her granddaughter, Jeanne Hegedus-Leary, married, she gave it to her as a wedding gift.

195. Yo-Yo; made by Edith Almann (b. 1926); Bronx County; 1934–1987; cotton; 85″ x 75″. (Collection of Edith Almann) The maker and owner of this quilt are the same person. She learned to quilt at home and started this quilt in 1934, when she was about seven years of age. This Yo-Yo pattern, a popular one in the 1930s, was her own idea, and she got most of the fabrics from Sears Roebuck, which sold them by the pound. Each circle is one inch wide and made from a two-inch fabric circle that is shirred in the center. The quilt contains 5,856 yo-yos, each of which took about three minutes to sew—a major project for a seven-year-old to undertake. Perhaps it was too large a project, for although the yo-yos were done by 1938, the maker notes that it actually took over fifty years to complete putting the quilt together. It was finally finished in July 1987.

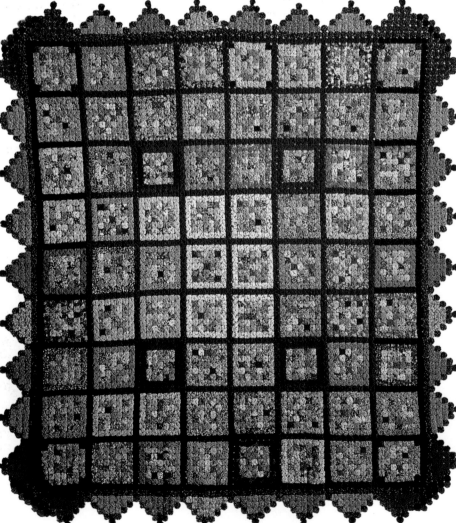

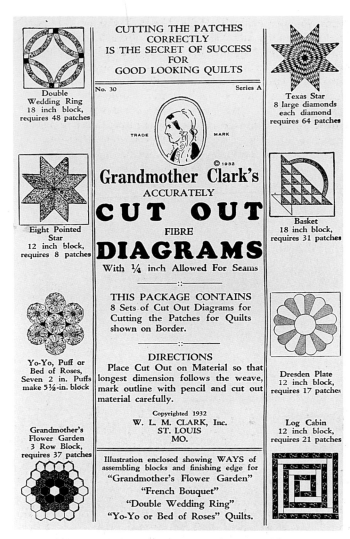

196. This cover illustration from a package of "Grandmother Clark's" quilt diagrams shows how women could purchase patterns earlier in this century. (Courtesy Alma Miller)

were actually registered in New York, and two of these, though of great beauty and craft, might only be considered borderline examples of the type. Ribbon quilts are somewhat analogous to strip quilts, only made from ribbons or "ribbons" of fabric—long, thin strips resembling ribbons. Apparently there was also a fad for ribbon quilts in England in the late nineteenth century—with the fabric of choice being the short lengths of ribbon used to trim hats—and it may have been this rage that was carried over to the States.[27] Quilts made entirely from ribbons have been found by quilt projects in other states, but none such as those were registered during the New York Quilt Days.

Around the turn of the century a simplified form of embroidered quilt began to capture the popular imagination. Square blocks of muslin stamped with designs for embroidery stitching (usually meant to be done in a chain or outline stitch) could be bought for a penny—complete with enough floss to complete the square—at local dry goods stores or at Woolworth's, then on its way to becoming a major chain outlet. When enough blocks had been purchased and embroidered, they would be sewn together, with or without sashing, to form what are now known as "penny-square" quilts, and a large number of these, from all parts of the state, were seen. Turkey Red or dark blue were the predominant colors used on the penny squares; squares done in pastel flosses occasionally turned up, but the deeper colors provided a more pleasing contrast and showed off the subject matter better.

Perhaps because penny squares seemed to be ideal mechanisms for teaching children the beginning fine points of stitching and embroidery, the stamped pictures tended to have more childlike themes. Favorite motifs included nursery rhymes, biblical stories, fairy tales, and

197. Laura Wheeler patterns were featured in newspapers like the *Buffalo Evening News.* (Courtesy Alma Miller)

198. Zodiac; made by Mabel Estelle Perry Smith (1878–1954); Rochester, Monroe County; 1937; pieced and appliquéd cotton; 97″ x 78″. (Collection of Dorothy Cunningham) Mabel Estelle Perry was born in Summit Station, New York, and married Norell Eugene Smith, store manager for the Grand Union Tea Company, on December 25, 1894. They lived in Syracuse, Elmira, Cortland, Rochester, and, in their later years, with a daughter in Binghamton. Mabel Smith was about sixty years old when she made this quilt, which is signed with her initials and its date of completion. Apparently this quilt design was created by "Nancy Page" (alias Florence LaGanke) and was offered one block at a time through newspapers throughout the country from October 1932 to January 1933.

199. Mabel Estelle Perry Smith (top row, second from right) and her family.

200. Pot of Flowers; made by Caroline Eppel Ayres (1866–1953); Rochester, Monroe County; c. 1920; appliquéd cotton; 81¼″ x 81¼″. (Collection of Elsbeth Wiegand-Starzynski) Caroline Eppel Ayres made quilts not only for family use but also to earn money for her family. She worked at the state hospital and her husband was a tailor, but extra money (they had five children, of whom two died at birth) was always useful. Her work was so well-known in Rochester that the *Rochester Democrat and Chronicle* featured her in its Sunday magazine on September 7, 1941. "She's been making quilts for over 70 years and still finds it more fun than anything. Her workshop is the great front room of the home in which she has lived for 41 years.... Much of the fun of making quilts for Mrs. Ayres is the designing of her own patterns.... 'It's something to look forward to; to sit down at the end of a hard day's work and see something not only beautiful but useful growing beneath my fingers. That's how I've always felt about quilting and always will feel, I guess.'"

201. Caroline Eppel Ayres (seated)

other children's stories, although historical and political figures and famous buildings have also been seen. The more artistic might even create their own designs or copy pictures from coloring books or elsewhere. Representations of buildings at the Pan American Exposition, as well as memorial portraits of McKinley noting his assassination there, were quite popular in 1901, and a number of quilts with the Exposition as a theme were seen during the Quilt Days. The enthusiasm for that topic quickly died, however, after the Exposition closed and became only an exciting and tragic memory.

The yo-yo quilts of the 1930s very often used small printed calicos, as is the case in the yo-yo quilt on page 130 that was started by a seven-year-old. Technically, a yo-yo work is not a quilt, because it is not a three-layered textile; nonetheless, it has become part of the quilting tradition. Its design sources have been traced back to the nineteenth century.[28] Today's sophisticated quilt textile artists look with disdain on the technique and it has decreased in general popularity as well, but to a youngster it was "fun to do" and served as a good introduction to sewing skills.

Perhaps the ubiquitousness of so many choices for quilt patterns and styles in the state can be partly attributed to the many resources that New York women had available to them. In earlier times, patterns were handed on from mother to daughter, neighbor to neighbor, but by the first quarter of the nineteenth century published patterns were beginning to be seen, and *Godey's Lady's Book* and *Harper's Bazar* played a major part in the spread of designs throughout the nation. The quilts shown at the numerous fairs and expositions within the state also served a function other than simple display. The prizewinning quilts were often viewed as the height of design and craftsmanship of the moment, and women would frequently copy the winning patterns in order to execute their own versions at home. This was one way in which designs were spread from one locale to another and might also explain why a rash of similar quilts might be found within a certain time period and region.

By this century, the transfer was done on an even broader scale, through pattern booklets and newspaper and magazine columns. Louise Fowler Roote, editor in the 1920s and 1930s of the Kate Marchbanks quilt column in *Capper's Weekly*, noted that she "haunted state fairs and quilting bees and teas" in the hope of finding new design sources for the column.[29] With the exception of a few backwater areas that had little access to modern technology and media, almost anyone anywhere could have easy access to hundreds of patterns, old and new, and this perhaps accounted for a certain rigidity that began to creep into many quilts that were made after about 1920. With so many choices at hand, it seemed, the desire to devise a variation on a theme—or a singular

202. Mountain Landscape; maker unknown; northern New York State; 1920–1930; cotton appliqué; 91½″ x 77″. (Collection of Shelburne Museum, Shelburne, Vermont) Pictorial quilts have become especially popular in this last quarter of the twentieth century, but such a specific scene as this one was rarely found in earlier years. Whether it represents nostalgia for bygone days or a rural fantasy will never be known. This quilt apparently has never been washed, for it retains the original glaze on the fabrics as well as the pencil marks the quilter made to assist her in quilting.

pattern—lessened, and many of the documented quilts from about that time on showed a certain loss of spontaneity and creativity. Printed designs and color suggestions were assiduously rather than informally or imaginatively followed, and it was a rare quilt that then stood out from the crowd.

The 1920s and 1930s in New York, as elsewhere, saw an abundance of elegant floral designs in soft pastels, patterns created by some of the best-known quilt designers of the day—delicate, delightful, and decorative, yet lacking the drama and power of many designs of earlier years. Yet, occasionally the mold would be broken, the prevailing fads of the day taken and turned upside-down, and the intrinsic independence of the New York woman would show itself in something characteristically her own.

And thus it continues—the comfort of the traditional, yet the elation of the pattern that breaks the norm, the design that turns a new corner. All this is inherent in the quilts of New York State and in their history—a history that is still unfolding and daily brings new insights and delights to the mind and the eye.

203. Pineapple; made by Nancy Margaret Helmer Folts (1832–1892); Kastbridge, Herkimer County; before 1900; appliquéd cotton; 85″ x 82″. (Collection of Madeline Helmer Fagan) The family of Nancy Margaret Helmer Folts was Palatine German and came to this country in the early eighteenth century; they were members of the Dutch and Reformed Church. The current owner, the great-granddaughter of the quiltmaker, has Nancy Folts's diaries and quilt patterns. The pineapple has long been the major symbol of hospitality in American decorative arts, where it is not only often found as a quilt motif but also used as finials on bed posts.

Appendix I: Quilt Guilds

The quilt guilds of New York State were the heart of the quilt-documentation search. This project could not have been accomplished without the superb organizational talents that the members of the guilds brought to this project. From the first public Quilt Day at Hempstead to the last public Quilt Day held in Dutchess County, they secured the physical space to run the day, publicized the event through local media, assisted in orienting the volunteers to do the oral interviews, photographed the quilts, and physically examined and described the quilts. This appendix is a special acknowledgment to all the guilds, their executive boards, memberships, and non-membership friends whom they drafted, for the commitment and dedication displayed.

Cuesta Benberry, the noted quilt historian, in a telephone interview in June 1991 with Jeanne Riger, supplied the following background about quilt guilds nationally. The Whitney Show of 1971 put quilts in a new and different context in this country. They now became viewed as art objects, and this view filtered down to the organizations that became quilt guilds. From the beginning, these guilds, many of them formed early in the 1970s, valued new ideas as well as the people who would teach new skills. About this time, a vital feminist movement put a new value on quilt making. The Hudson River Valley Quilt made by a group of concerned quilters tied this to the rising ecology movement. New quilt books were written, for most of the old quilt books had gone out of print. Robert Bishop and Carleton Safford published *America's Quilts and Coverlets* in 1972, and Patsy and Myron Orlofsky published *Quilts in America* in 1974. Both books incorporated this new emphasis. Workshops were held that were open to new ideas. The aim of the guilds was to pull in many more people than could sit around a quilting frame. There were study groups that met monthly to listen to lectures and watch new techniques. Many guilds had spin-off clubs of women who wanted to sew and quilt. A Continental Quilting Congress was held and a Quilter's Hall of Fame was established. The New England Quilters Guild was organized and other regional groups developed.

The guilds are formally organized and each has a constitution or by-laws. They collect dues and publish newsletters. Important in their organization is the program chairperson, who develops serious programs. They have developed a coterie of national teachers who are responsible for workshops and travel across the country teaching new techniques.

New York State has the distinction of having the oldest quilt-study club in the United States, the Genesee Valley Quilt Association, which was founded by Gladys Reid Holton on January 30, 1936 at the request of the Rochester Museum of Arts and Science. Today, the state also has an extensive guild system with networking both intrastate and interstate. Thus, in setting documentation days for the New York Quilt Project, it was possible to establish regions headed by regional coordinators who worked with local area coordinators having ties to local quilt guilds.

NY/Pa Consortium (organized in 1986) covers the area of the state from Watertown west to Olean and south to the Pennsylvania border. The consortium acts as a networking organization and publishes a newsletter. Consortium guilds sponsoring Quilt Days were Common Threads Quilt Guild (organized in 1983) acting with Stepping Stones Guild (date of organization unknown) and Valley Quilters (organized in the 1970s), Diane Sutherland and Joan Shaver, local coordinators; Corning Quilters Guild (organized in 1974), Vida Johnson, local coordinator; Genesee Valley Quilt Association (organized in 1936), Karen LaDuca, local coordinator; Mohawk Valley Quilt Club (organized in 1979), Linda Hazelden, local coordinator; Plankroad Quilt Guild (organized in 1982), jointly with Towpath Quilt Guild (organized in 1981), Linda Meyer, Mary Helen Foster, and Cele Rosenthal, local coordinators; Susquehanna Valley Quilters (organized in the 1980s), Jeannine Petersen, local coordinator; Thumbstall Quilt Guild, (organized in 1976), Anne Legg, local coordinator; and Tompkins County Quilters Guild, Inc. (organized in 1976), Alanna Fontanella, local coordinator. Members of other guilds in the consortium participated in various Quilt Days even when their own guild was not a sponsor. Other members of the consortium are Candlelight Quilters Guild, Baldwinsville;

Irondequoit Quilt Club, suburban Rochester; Lake Country Quilt Guild, Fulton; Lake-To-Lake Quilters, Gorham; Park Patches Quilt Guild, Hornell-Olean; Piecemakers Quilters, Elmira; Piecemakers Quilt Guild, Ilion; and Southern Tier Quilt Guild, Olean. Diane Sutherland was the NYQP regional coordinator for all the guilds in the Consortium.

In the western region of New York State, Nancilu Burdick, the regional coordinator, enlisted the aid of the Amherst Museum Quilters Guild (organized in 1975), Nancy Heintz, local coordinator; and Kenan Quilter's Guild (organized in 1985), Linda Davis, local coordinator. With the help of Barbara Phillippi in Belfast, Joanne Langham in Jamestown, and Nancy Hoyler in Hamburg, five Quilt Days were held staffed by individual quilters. The Buffalo and Erie County Historical Society collection of quilts were documented by Nancilu Burdick, Michelle Fitch and Barbara Nagle.

The North Country region was coordinated by Edith Mitchell with the aid of Champlain Valley Quilters of New York State (date of organization unknown), Sally White, local coordinator; North Country Quilter Guild (date of organization unknown), Patricia Finnerty, local coordinator; Raquette River Quilters (organized in 1981); and Wings Falls Quilter's Guild (organized in 1977), Jan Spielberger, local coordinator.

In the Catskill region, Anna Marie Tucker, regional coordinator, worked with the Delaware County Historical Quilters (organized in 1976) and Delaware County Town and Country Quilters (organized in 1988), Marilyn Guy and Lois Gould, local coordinators; and many individual quilters drawn from small quilting groups. Calico Geese Quilters of Sullivan County (organized in 1986), Beatrice Rexford, local coordinator, held the Quilt Day for that section of the Catskills.

Individual guilds in the Hudson Valley coordinating Quilt Days were: First Dutchess Quilters, Inc. (organized in 1975), Arlene Hodgeman, local coordinator; Heritage Quilters of the Hudson Palisades (date of organization unknown), Joyce Rizzuto, local coordinator; Northern Star Quilters' Guild, Ltd. (organized in 1981), Penny Black, local coordinator; The Wiltwyck Quilters Guild of Ulster County (organized in 1977), Marge Holsapple, local coordinator, and The Warwick Valley Quilters' Guild (organized in 1982), Phyllis Klein, local coordinator, Orange County. Individual quilters were coordinated by Betty Monahan in Marlboro, Ulster County.

In the metropolitan region, New York County was coordinated by the Empire Quilters (organized in 1982), Helen Tiger, local coordinator; and Kings County was coordinated by the Brooklyn Quilters (organized in 1982), Donna DeFalco Boyle, local coordinator.

Nassau County was coordinated by the Long Island Quilter's Society, Inc. (organized in 1976), Kathee Versheck, Janet Ratner, and Margot Cohen, local coordinators.

Suffolk County was coordinated by Eastern Long Island Quilter's Guild (organized in 1981), Aurelie Stack, Regional Coordinator.

All the guilds offer their memberships social fellowship, education in the history and craft of quilting, opportunities to exhibit their own work and trips to quilt conventions and exhibits. As they have matured, many have become involved in charitable and community causes. They make and contribute quilts to AIDS babies, nursing homes, senior citizen centers, Ronald McDonald Houses, battered women's shelters and shelters for the homeless, as well as fundraising quilts for churches, local arts groups and educational institutions.

Appendix II: List of Quilt Days

Date	Site and Sponsor	No. of Quilts

March 26, 1988   Hofstra University, Hempstead; Long Island Quilter's Society.   **102**

April 23, 1988   State University of New York, Stony Brook; SUNY Crafts Center, Marcia Wiener, Director.   **121**

June 18, 1988   Southold Recreation Center, Peconic; Eastern Long Island Quilter's Guild and Cutchogue–New Suffolk Historical Council, George Brown, President.   **128**

August 7, 1988   East Hampton Middle School, East Hampton; Eastern Long Island Quilter's Guild and East Hampton Historical Society.   **119**

September 10, 1988   Suffolk County Historical Society, Riverhead; Wallace W. Broege, Director, and Eastern Long Island Quilter's Guild.   **120**

October 1, 1988   Oysterponds Historical Society, Orient; Jean Martin, Director, and Eastern Long Island Quilter's Guild.   **186**

October 15, 1988   Parrish Art Museum, Southampton; Melissa Patton, Curator of Education, and Eastern Long Island Quilter's Guild.   **120**

November 5, 1988   Museum of the City of New York, Manhattan; Robert R. Macdonald, Director.   **77**

February 4, 1989   St. James Cathedral, Brooklyn; Brooklyn Quilters.   **64**

March 18, 1989   Somers Intermediate School, Somers; Northern Star Quilters' Guild, Ltd.   **72**

April 8, 1989   Rockland County Cornell Cooperative Extension, Thiells; Kermit W. Graf, Director, and Heritage Quilters of Hudson Palisades.   **51**

April 15, 1989   Marlboro Elementary School, Marlboro; Elizabeth Mannion, Marlboro Librarian, and Betty Monahan.   **135**

April 17 and 18, 1989   Warnerville Methodist Church, Warnerville; Rev. Victor and Mrs. Lee Zaccaro, and local quilters.   **135**

May 13, 1989   Christ Episcopal Church, Warwick; Warwick Valley Quilters' Guild.   **132**

May 16 and 17, 1989   St. George's Episcopal Church, Schenectady; Rev. Marshall J. Vang and Sybil Telfian, and local quilters.   **142**

May 19 and 20, 1989   Amherst Colony Museum, Amherst; Dr. Andrea Shaw, Director, and Amherst Museum Quilters Guild.   **223**

May 20, 1989   Erie County Fairgrounds, Hamburg; Colden Valley Quilt Shop (Nancy Hoyler), and local quilters.   **123**

June 7, 1989   Delaware County Cornell Cooperative Extension, Hamden; Jeanne Darling, County Agent, and Delaware County Town and Country Quilters.   **74**

June 10, 1989   Buffalo–Erie County Historical Society, Buffalo; Dr. William Siener, Director, Museum staff and docents, and Kenan Quilter's Guild.   **206**

June 12, 1989   Allegany County Cornell Cooperative Extension, Municipal Building, Belfast; Charles Clark, Town Supervisor, and Barbara Phillippi.   **269**

June 14 and 17, 1989   Niagara County Cornell Cooperative Extension, Lockport; John Mulcahy, Coordinator, and Kenan Quilter's Guild.   **374**

June 23 and 24, 1989   Margaret Woodbury Strong Museum, Rochester; G. Rollie Adams, President, and Genesee Valley Quilt Guild.   **378**

July 11, 1989   Schweinfurth Art Center, Auburn, Lisa Pennella, Director, and Thumbstall Quilters Guild.   **107**

July 15, 1989   Sullivan County Cornell Cooperative Extension, Liberty; Calico Geese Quilters of Sullivan County.   **192**

July 25, 1989   YWCA, Jamestown; Pat Smith, and Joanne Langham of Calico Cat.   **83**

August 19, 1989   Ulster County Community College, Stone Ridge; Dean Donald Katt and Ms. Pat Yeager, and Wiltwyck Quilters Guild.   **164**

September 9 and 10, 1989   WCNY Public TV Station, Syracuse; Richard Calagiovanni, Manager, and Plankroad Quilt Guild and Towpath Quilt Guild.   **315**

September 16, 1989   Ithaca High School, Ithaca; Carol Pagliaro, and Tompkins County Quilt Guild.   **217**

September 21, 1989   County Office Building, Owego; Valley Quilters.   **127**

September 23, 1989   Calvary Methodist Church, Vestal; Common Threads Quilt Guild and Stepping Stones Guild.   **132**

September 30, 1989   SUNY, Utica; Mohawk Valley Quilt Club.   **289**

October 7, 1989   St. James Episcopal Church, Oneonta; Rev. Richard Frye, and Susquehanna Valley Quilters.   **133**

October 14, 1989   Corning–Painted Post West High School, Corning; Corning Quilters Guild.   **119**

October 19, 1989   Potsdam Public Museum, Potsdam; Betsy Travis, Director, museum personnel and local quilters.   **109**

October 20, 1989   Old Courthouse, Plattsburgh; Champlain Valley Quilters of New York.   **57**

October 21, 1989   Jefferson County Cooperative Extension, Watertown; North Country Quilters.   **90**

November 3, 1989   Ivy Terrace Senior Citizens Center, Tupper Lake; Raquette River Quilters.   **86**

November 4, 1989   Church of the Messiah, Glens Falls; Wings Falls Quilter's Guild.   **99**

November 11, 1989   Oak Grove Grange Hall, Wappinger Falls; Emma Buck, and First Dutchess Quilters.   **116**

A total of 5,786 quilts were documented at these public quilt days. Additional quilts were documented through the mails and at dealers and private collections, adding up to more than 6,000 at time of publication.

Notes

Introduction

1. Louis C. Jones, *Three Eyes on the Past: Exploring New York Folk Life* (Syracuse, N.Y.: Syracuse University Press, 1982), 11–12.

2. Marsha MacDowell and C. Kurt Dewhurst, "Expanding Frontiers: The Michigan Folk Art Project," in *Perspectives on American Folk Art*, edited by Ian M. G. Quimby and Scott T. Swank (New York: W. W. Norton and Company, 1980), 59.

Images of the Past

1. David M. Ellis, James A. Frost, Harold C. Syrett, and Harry I. Carmen, *A History of New York State* (Ithaca: Cornell University Press, 1967), 21.

2. Alexander C. Flick, ed., *History of the State of New York in Ten Volumes*, 3 (New York: Columbia University Press and the New York State Historical Association, 1935), 94.

3. From Rev. Clement Cruttwell, *The New Universal Gazetteer, or Geographical Dictionary*, 4 vols. (London: Longman, Hurst, Rees, and Orme, 1808), under "York (New)" in 4.

4. Ellis, et al., *A History of New York State*, 28.

5. Sherman Williams, *New York's Part in History* (New York: D. Appleton & Co., 1915), 219.

6. John H. Thompson, ed., *Geography of New York State* (Syracuse: Syracuse University Press, 1966), 140–42.

7. Ibid., 168.

8. George H. Warner, *Military Records of Schoharie Veterans of Four Wars* (Albany: privately published, 1891), 73.

9. Ibid., 82.

10. Arch Merrill, *The Towpath* (Rochester: Creek Books, 1945), 17–18.

11. See Ellis et al., *A History of New York State*, 281; Cruttwell, *The New Universal Gazetteer*, 4.

12. Edwin Robb Ellis, *The Epic of New York City* (New York: Coward-McCann, 1966), 262–265.

13. Telephone conversations with Wesley Prieb, Curator of Historical Collections, Tabor College, Hillsboro, Kans., August 1991.

14. Winthrop S. Hudson, *Religion in America*, 2d ed. (New York: Charles Scribner's Sons, 1973), 146.

15. From the "Proceedings," Grand Lodge, New York, 1920, 136, as quoted in Robert Ingham Clegg, *Mackey's History of Freemasonry*, 7 (Chicago: The Masonic History Company, 1921), 2054.

16. Although New York had organized a general chapter of the Eastern Star in 1870, it was not founded as a national society until 1876. Clegg, *Mackey's History of Freemasonry*, 2004.

17. Marion F. Noyes, ed. *A History of Schoharie County* (Schoharie, N.Y.: Schoharie County Historical Society, 1980), 39.

18. Ellis et al., *A History of New York State*, 339–341.

19. George Winston Smith and Charles Judah, *Life in the North During the Civil War: A Source History* (Albuquerque: University of New Mexico Press, 1966), 167.

20. *Moore's Rural-New Yorker*, 4 March 1865, 71: "Now that cotton is scarce and high, it seems more necessary than ever that old bed quilts should be saved to cover, line and quilt again.... When ready to quilt, first tack your lining to four quilt frames so that it will be smooth, then spread on the old quilt and baste fast to the lining on frames; over this spread the outside, and fasten the edges, having all parts smooth. The cotton is kept in place by the quilting in the old quilt. It is not necessary to put as much work on the new quilt. A lady who quilted one thus, about three inches apart, put it on, quilted, took it off and bound it in two days, doing all the work herself except assistance in rolling. And she had a thicker, warmer quilt than the old one."

21. Caroline Cowles Richards, *Village Life in America, 1852–1872* (New York: Henry Holt and Company, 1908), 199.

22. William Howell Reed, *The Heroic Story of the U. S. Sanitary Commission, 1861–1865* (Boston: G. H. Ellis, n.d.).

23. For more detailed information on the Sanitary Commission, see, for example, Reed, ibid., and James M. McPherson, *Battle Cry of Freedom: The Civil War Era* (New York: Oxford University Press, 1988). Reed has also noted that, "The service to the nation rendered by the United States Sanitary Commission during the Civil War is hardly known to present generations and is almost forgotten."

24. Virginia Gunn, "Quilts for Union Soldiers in the Civil War," *Uncoverings 1985*, 6 (Mill Valley, Calif.: American Quilt Study Group, 1986), 106.

25. As quoted in ibid., 113.

26. See, for example, Gen. George W. Davies, "The Sanitary Commission—Red Cross," *Journal of International Law*, July 1910, and Charles Hurd, *The Compact History of the American Red Cross* (New York: Hawthorn Books, 1959).

27. Ellis et al., *A History of New York State*, 512.

28. Ibid., 627. Lillian Russell was born in Clinton, Iowa, December 4, 1861, and raised in Chicago. Her mother was a feminist and active in the women's suffrage movement; at various times she ran a project to rehabilitate prostitutes, wrote novels, and established schools and temporary churches.

Russell's father was a printer and atheist. Lillian Russell was a concert-hall singer by the age of sixteen; she came to New York to study opera but instead took up the life of a chorus girl and gained both fame and notoriety during her long theatrical career.

29. Richard Lowitt and Maurine Beasley, eds., *One Third of a Nation: Lorena Hickok Reports on the Great Depression* (Urbana, Ill.: University of Illinois Press, 1981), xvii-xxxv.

30. In a letter to Hopkins 12–19 September 1933, as quoted in ibid., 28.

31. Jeanne Westin, *Making Do: How Women Survived the '30s* (Chicago: Follett Publishing Company, 1976), 11.

32. Ibid., 283.

Images in Fabric

1. Kax Wilson, *A History of Textiles* (Boulder, Colo.: Westview Press, 1979), 233–250.

2. Ibid., 235.

3. Ibid., 236.

4. Bagnall, as quoted in ibid., 236.

5. Jared Van Wagenen, Jr., *The Golden Age of Homespun* (Ithaca: Cornell University Press, 1960), 249.

6. Helen G. and Andrus T. Valentine, *An Island's People: One Foot in the Sea, One on Shore* (Huntington, N.Y.: Peterson Press and Associates, 1976), 89–90.

7. Jeannette Edwards Rattray, *East Hampton History, Including Genealogies of Early Families* (Garden City, N.Y.: privately printed, 1953).

8. As recorded in Benjamin F. Thompson, *History of Long Island From its Discovery and Settlement to the Present Time*, 3d ed. 2 (New York: Robert H. Dodd, 1918).

9. See, for example, Clayton Mau, *The Development of Central and Western New York: From the Arrival of the White Man to the Eve of the Civil War*, rev. ed. (Dansville, N.Y.: F.A. Owen Publishing Company, 1958), 90, and Andrew W. Young, *History of Chautauqua County* (Buffalo: 1876), 82–83.

10. Wilson, *History of Textiles*.

11. David M. Ellis, James A. Frost, Harold C. Syrett, and Harry I. Carmen, *A History of New York State* (Ithaca, N.Y.: Cornell University Press, 1967), 183.

12. Frank L. Walton, *Tomahawks to Textiles: The Fabulous Story of Worth Street* (New York: Appleton-Century-Crofts, 1953), 98.

13. Alexander C. Flick, ed. *History of the State of New York in Ten Volumes*, 6 (New York: Columbia University Press and the New York State Historical Association, 1935), 194.

14. "General Store Operations," *Heritage* 7, no. 6 (July/August 1991).

15. Flick, *History of the State of New York*, 6, 198.

16. "General Store Operations," *Heritage* 7, no. 6 (July/August 1991).

17. Walton, *Tomahawks to Textiles*, 102.

18. Rev. Clement Cruttwell, *The New Universal Gazetteer, or Geographical Dictionary*, 4 vols. (London: Longman, Hurst, Rees, and Orme, 1808), under "York (New)" 4, unpaged.

19. Ellis et al., *A History of New York State*, 175.

20. Fran Lieu, "Candace Thurber Wheeler," Folk Art Institute, Museum of American Folk Art, Spring 1991, 1-11.

21. Wilson, *History of Textiles*, 243.

22. Ibid.

23. Florence H. Pettit, *America's Printed and Painted Fabrics: 1600-1900* (New York: Hastings House, 1970), 23.

24. Ibid., 67-69.

25. Mary Schoeser and Celia Rufey, *English and American Textiles from 1790 to the Present* (New York: Thames & Hudson, 1989), 76.

26. Ibid.

27. Barbara Brackman, *Clues in the Calico* (McLean, Va.: EPM Publications, 1989), 86–87.

28. *The Blue Book Textile Directory of the United States and Canada*, 1 (New York, Davidson Publishing, 1899-1940).

29. Van Wagenen, *The Golden Age of Homespun*, 181–182. He notes that "... the sum total [production] of 1,439 pounds for the entire state must be regarded as insignificant.... Some hardy and optimistic experimentalist of Chenango County reported a yield of one pound of silk, which represented the entire production of his county."

30. "General Store Operations," *Heritage* 7, no. 6 (July/August 1991).

31. Papers of Abiathar Watkins and His Wife Emily L., 1836-1894, Manuscript Collection of the New York Public Library.

32. Mrs. Pullan, *The Lady's Manual of Fancy Work* (New York: 1858), 95.

33. Virginia Gunn, "Dress Fabrics of the Late Nineteenth Century," in Jeannette Lasansky et al., *Bits and Pieces: Textile Traditions* (Lewisburg, Pa.: Oral Traditions Project of the Union Historical Project, 1991), 4-15.

34. *Harper's Bazar*, November 2, 1867.

35. Wilson, *History of Textiles*, 240.

Images of Woman

1. Letter, Abigail Adams to John Adams, 31 March 1776; Massachusetts Historical Society, Boston.

2. Jill K. Conway, *The Female Experience in 18th and 19th Century America: A Guide to the History of American Women* (Princeton: Princeton University Press, 1982), xxiii.

3. Susan Burrows Swan, *Plain & Fancy: American Women and Their Needlework, 1700–1850* (New York: Holt, Rinehart & Winston, 1977), 192.

4. As quoted in Gail Andrews Trechsel, "Mourning Quilts in America," *Uncoverings 1989*, 140.

5. Ibid., 141.

6. The Diaries of Caroline A. Dunstan, 1856-1870. Manuscript Division of the Research Libraries of the New York Public Library; entries for 15 and 18 April 1865.

7. Ibid., 31 March 1869.

8. Jane Bentley Kolter, in *Forget Me Not: A Gallery of Friendship and Album Quilts* (Pittstown, N.J.: The Main Street Press, 1985), remarks that a "number of towns in central New York produced Chimney Sweep quilts with dark-ground printed textiles," thus making them readily identifiable as to region of origin (59).

9. Probably the best-known and most common of these books from about 1840 until the end of the century, and a possible source for these verses, was *Songs, Divine and Moral, for the Use of Children*, by the Reverend Isaac Watts. See Toni Flores Fratto, "Remember Me: The Sources of American Sampler Verses," *New York Folklore* 2, Winter 1976, 205–222.

10. Ethel Stanwood Bolton and Eva Johnston Coe, *American Samplers* (New York: Weathervane Books, 1973), 372.

11. Marion F. Noyes, "Early Academies and Seminaries of Schoharie County," unpublished master's thesis, 1938, 7.

12. Required days of schooling varied considerably. William Bouck, later a governor of the state, attended the first school in Schoharie County established under this law; his attendance record of 59 days for the year was the best of any student in the school. From Marion F. Noyes, ed., *A History of Schoharie County* (Schoharie, N.Y.: Schoharie County Historical Society, 1964, 1980), 100.

13. C. Kurt Dewhurst, Betty MacDowell, and Marsha MacDowell, *Religious Folk Art in America: Reflections of Faith* (New York: E.P. Dutton in association with the Museum of American Folk Art, 1983), 35.

14. David M. Ellis, James A. Frost, Harold C. Syrett, and Harry I. Carmen, *A History of New York State* (Ithaca: Cornell University Press, 1967), 321.

15. Noyes, *A History of Schoharie County*, 104.

16. Noyes, "Early Academies and Seminaries," 34.

17. Ibid., 10.

18. Mrs. Child, *The Little Girl's Own Book*, 1840.

19. Caroline Cowles Richards, entry for September 1, 1854, *Village Life in America, 1852–1872* (New York: Henry Holt and Company, 1908), 39–40.

20. Helen Doyle, *A Child Went Forth: The Autobiography of Dr. Helen McKnight* (New York: Gotham House, 1934), 45.

21. Jeannette Edwards Rattray, *East Hampton History, Including Genealogy of Early Families* (Garden City, N.Y.: privately printed, 1953), 46.

22. "Orphelina: A Tale by Miss Leslie," in *Miss Leslie's Magazine*, 1, March 1843.

23. As quoted in Barbara M. Cross, ed., *The Autobiography of Lyman Beecher*, 1 (Massachusetts: Harvard University Press, 1961), 98.

24. Susan Burrows Swan, *Plain and Fancy: American Women and their Needlework, 1700–1850* (New York: Holt, Rinehart & Winston, 1977).

25. *The Cultivator*, 4, April 1837, 43.

26. *The Young Lady's Friend*, 1837, 41.

27. Julia McNair Wright, *The Complete Home: An Encyclopedia of Domestic Life and Affairs* (Philadelphia: J.C. McCurdy & Co., 1879), 563.

28. Bette S. Werdman and Linda B. Martin, *Nassau County, Long Island, in Early Photographs: 1869–1940* (New York: Dover, 1981), 51.

29. Barbara Brackman, "Fairs and Expositions: Their Influence on American Quilts," in Jeannette Lasansky et al., *Bits and Pieces: Textile Traditions* (Lewisburg Pa.: Oral Traditions Project of the Union Historical Project, 1991), 90–99.

30. See, for example, David M. Ellis, James A. Frost, Harold C. Syrett, and Harry I. Carmen, *A History of New York State* (Ithaca: Cornell University Press, 1967), 171, and John B. Howe, *The New York State Fair: Its Genesis and Its History* (Syracuse: Hall & McChesney, 1917), 8.

31. Henry W. Schramm, *Empire Show Case: A History of the New York State Fair* (Utica, N.Y.: North Country Books, 1985), 8.

32. *The Cultivator*, October 1844, 11, no. 10, 312.

33. Ibid., October 1846, 3 (New Series), 10, 321.

34. Mary A. de Julio, "What a Rich Reward! Betsey Reynolds Voorhees and the Collection of Her Handiwork," Exhibition Catalogue of the Montgomery County Historical Society (Fort Johnson, N.Y. 1986), 19.

35. Ibid., 66.

36. As quoted in Frances Lichten, *Decorative Art of Victoria's Era* (New York: Charles Scribner's Sons, 1950), 92.

37. Ibid., 563–64.

38. Susan Strasser, *Never Done: A History of American Housework* (New York: Pantheon Books, 1982), 125–134.

39. Sarah M. Lockwood, as quoted in Gertrude Whiting, *Tools and Toys of Stitchery* (New York: Columbia University Press, 1928).

40. *Moore's Rural New-Yorker*, 23 September 1854, 303.

41. "Sewing Machines for the Farmer's Family," *Moore's Rural New-Yorker*, 2 January 1858, 6.

42. "What a Farmer's Girl Should Know," *Moore's Rural New-Yorker*, 31 January 1863. The piece suggested that the girl should also know how to sing and play the melodeon!

43. Suellen Meyer, "Early Influences of the Sewing Machine and Visible Machine Stitching on Nineteenth-Century Quilts," *Uncoverings 1989*, 10 (San Francisco: American Quilt Study Group, 1990), 46.

44. Ibid.

45. *Harper's Bazar*, 7 December 1867, 87.

46. Alexander C. Flick, ed., *History of the State of New York*, 8 (New York: Columbia University Press, 1935), 325.

47. "Twin Counties Mark Two Hundred Years," *Heritage* 7, no. 6 (July/August 1991).

48. Katharine Anthony, *Susan B. Anthony: Her Personal History and Her Era* (Garden City, N.Y.: Doubleday & Co., 1954), 37.

49. See *The Southold Sisterhood—Sociables and Serious Business: The Story of the Ladies Liberal Sewing Society of the First Universalist Church of Southold, New York in 1845*, an interpretive journal based on the twenty-two handwritten volumes of minutes and treasurer's books of the Ladies Society.

50. The Diaries of Caroline A. Dunstan, 1856–1870. Manuscript Division of the Research Libraries of the New York Public Library.

Images in the Making

1. Barbara Brackman, *Clues in the Calico* (McLean, Va.: EPM Publications, 1989), 169.

2. Ibid., 168.

3. Sybil Lanigan, "The Revival of the Patchwork Quilt," *Ladies' Home Journal*, October 1894, 19.

4. Phyllis Haders, *The Warner's Collector's Guide to American Quilts* (Pittstown, N.J.: Main Street Press, 1981), 156.

5. Brackman, *Clues in the Calico*, 168.

6. Ibid., 170.

7. See, for example, Amelia Peck, *Quilts and Coverlets in the Collection of the Metropolitan Museum of Art* (New York: Metropolitan Museum of Art and Dutton Studio Books, 1990), 65; Janet Rae, *Quilts of the British Isles* (New York: E.P. Dutton, 1987), 68; and Averil Colby, *Patchwork* (New York: P. T. Batsford, 1958), 66.

8. Jane Bentley Kolter, *Forget Me Not: A Gallery of Friendship and Album Quilts* (Pittstown, N.J.: The Main Street Press, 1985), 9.

9. Miss Florence Hartley, *Ladies Hand Book of Fancy and Ornamental Work* (Philadelphia, 1859).

10. Brackman, *Clues in the Calico*, 155–156.

11. Ibid., 158.

12. Dolores Hinson, *Quilting Manual* (New York: Dover Publications, 1966), 14. See also Lynn Steuer, unpublished manuscript, Folk Art Institute, Museum of American Folk Art, Spring, 1991.

13. Carrie A. Hall and Rose G. Kretsinger. *The Romance of the Patchwork Quilt in America in Three Parts* (New York: Bonanza Books, 1935), 125.

14. Carleton L. Safford and Robert Bishop, *America's Quilts and Coverlets* (New York: Bonanza Books, 1985), 291.

15. According to Phillip H. Curtis, in "American Quilts in the Newark Museum Collection" (*The Museum New Series* 25, nos. 3–4, Summer-Fall 1973), "There are over 46 recorded quilt names with religious connotations." 9.

16. Judy Mathieson, "Some Published Sources of Design Inspiration for the Quilt Pattern Mariner's Compass—17th to 20th Century," *Uncoverings 1981* (Mill Valley, Calif.: American Quilt Study Group, 1982), 11–17.

17. Jean Taylor Federico, "White Work Classification System," *Uncoverings 1980* (Mill Valley, Calif.: American Quilt Study Group, 1981), 68.

18. See Florence Montgomery, *Textiles in America: 1650–1870* (New York: W.W. Norton & Co., 1984), 185–187; and *Fairchild's Dictionary of Textiles*, edited by Dr. Isabel B. Wingate (New York: Fairchild Publications, Inc., 1974), 95.

19. Allan I. Ludwig, *Graven Images: New England Stonecarving and Its Symbols, 1650–1815* (Middletown, Conn.: Wesleyan University Press, 1966), 109.

20. Suellen Meyer, "Pine Tree Quilts," *Quilt Digest* 4 (San Francisco: Quilt Digest Press, 1986), 16. See also Jared Van Wagenen, Jr., *The Golden Age of Homespun* (Ithaca, N.Y.: Cornell University Press, 1960), 142, 159.

21. Penny McMorris, *Crazy Quilts* (New York: E. P. Dutton, 1984).

22. Ibid., 12.

23. "Home Decorative Notes," *The Real Estate Record and Guide*, 31 January 1885, 104.

24. From *The Ohio Farmer*, 4 February 1882, as cited in McMorris, *Crazy Quilts*, 82.

25. From "Crazy Work and Sane Work," *Harpers Bazar*, 13 September 1884, 17, no. 37, 578–579.

26. "Home Decorative Notes," *The Real Estate Record and Guide*, 14 November 1885, 1249.

27. Conversation with Barbara Brackman, 17 August 1991. See also Pamela Clabburn, *Album Patchwork* (Aylesbury, Bucks, U.K.: Shire Publications Ltd., 1983), 6.

28. Virginia Gunn, "Yo-Yo or Bed of Roses Quilts: Nineteenth Century Origins," *Uncoverings 1987* (Mill Valley, Calif.: American Quilt Study Group, 1988), 129–146.

29. Louise Fowler Roote, *Kate's Blue Ribbon Quilts* (Topeka, Kan.: Capper's Publications, c. 1971), 2. As cited in Barbara Brackman, "Fairs and Expositions," in Jeannette Lasansky et al., *Bits and Pieces: Textile Traditions* (Lewisburg, Pa.: An Oral Traditions Project of the Union County Historical Society, 1991), 98.

Bibliography

Books:

Ahlstrom, Sydney E. *A Religious History of the American People*. Garden City, N.Y.: Doubleday & Co., 1975.

Anthony, Katharine. *Susan B. Anthony: Her Personal History and her Era*. Garden City, N.Y.: Doubleday & Co., 1954.

Asbury, Herbert. *The Great Illusion: An Informal History of Prohibition*. Garden City, N.Y.: Doubleday & Co., 1950.

Barthel, Diane L. *Amana: From Pietist Sect to American Community*. Lincoln, Neb.: University of Nebraska Press, 1984.

Bayles, Richard M. *Historical and Descriptive Sketches of Suffolk County with a Historical Outline of Long Island*. Port Washington, N.Y.: Empire State Historical Publication XVII, 1962.

Bishop, Robert. *New Discoveries in American Quilts*. New York: E. P. Dutton & Co., 1975.

————, and Patricia Coblentz. *American Decorative Arts: 360 Years of Creative Design*. New York: Harry N. Abrams, 1982.

————, William Secord, and Judith Reiter Weissman. *Quilts, Coverlets, Rugs and Samplers*. New York: Alfred A. Knopf, 1982.

Bolton, Ethel Stanwood, and Eva Johnston Coe. *American Samplers*. New York: Weathervane Books, 1973.

Brackman, Barbara. *Clues in the Calico*. McLean, Va.: EPM Publications, 1989.

————, "Fairs and Expositions: Their Influence on American Quilts." In *Bits and Pieces: Textile Traditions*. Edited by Jeannette Lasansky. Lewisburg, Pa.: Oral Traditions Project of the Union County Historical Society, 1991.

Brandon, Ruth. *A Capitalist Romance: Singer and the Sewing Machine*. Philadelphia: J. B. Lippincott, 1977.

Braunlein, John H. *Colonial Long Island Folklife*. Stony Brook, N.Y.: The Museums at Stony Brook, 1976.

Bresenhan, Karoline Patterson, and Nancy O'Bryant Puentes. *Lone Stars: A Legacy of Texas Quilts, 1836–1936*. Austin, Tex.: University of Texas Press, 1986.

Bussing, Ann Van Nest. *Reminiscences of the Van Nest Homestead*. New York: privately published, 1897.

Christensen, Erwin O. *The Index of American Design*. New York: Macmillan, 1950.

Clabburn, Pamela. *Shire 101 Album Patchwork*. Aylesbury, Bucks, United Kingdom: Shire Publications Ltd., 1983.

Clegg, Robert Ingham. *Mackey's History of Freemasonry*, Vol. 6, Chicago: The Masonic History Company, 1921.

Coffin, Margaret. *The History and Folklore of American Country Tinware 1700–1900*. New York: Galahad Books, 1968.

Cogan, Frances B. *All American Girl: The Ideal of Real Womanhood in Mid-Nineteenth-Century America*. Athens, Ga.: University of Georgia Press, 1989.

Colby, Averil. *Patchwork*. New York: P. T. Batsford, 1958.

Conway, Jill K. *The Female Experience in Eighteenth and Nineteenth Century America*. Princeton: Princeton University Press, 1985.

Cross, Barbara M., ed. *The Autobiography of Lyman Beecher*, Vol. 1. Cambridge: Harvard University Press, 1961.

Cruttwell, Rev. Clement. *The New Universal Gazetteer, or Geographical Dictionary*. 4 vols. London: Longman, Hurst, Rees, and Orme, 1808.

Dannett, Sylvia, ed. *Noble Women of the North*. New York: Thomas Yoseloff, 1959.

Davidson, Marshall B. *A Pictorial History of New York*. New York: Charles Scribner's Sons, 1977.

Davis, Mildred J. *The Art of Crewel Embroidery*. New York: Crown Publishers, 1962.

Dewhurst, C. Kurt, Betty MacDowell, and Marsha MacDowell. *Religious Folk Art in America: Reflections of Faith*. New York: E. P. Dutton, 1983.

Douglas, Ann. *The Feminization of American Culture*. New York: Alfred A. Knopf, 1978.

Doyle, Helen. *A Child Went Forth: The Autobiography of Dr. Helen McKnight*. New York: Gotham House, 1934.

Dumenil, Lynn. *Freemasonry and American Culture, 1880–1930*. Princeton, N.J.: Princeton University Press, 1984.

Dunbaugh, Edwin L. "New York to Boston via the Long Island Railroad." In *Long Island Studies: Evoking a Sense of Place*. Edited by Joann P. Krieg. Interlaken, N.Y.: Heart of the Lakes Publishing, 1988.

Ellis, David M., James A. Frost, Harold C. Syrett and Harry I. Carmen. *A History of New York State*. Ithaca, N.Y.: Cornell University Press, 1967.

Ellis, Edwin Robb. *The Epic of New York City*. New York: Coward-McCann, 1966.

Failey, Dean F. *Long Island Is My Nation: The Decorative Arts & Craftsmen, 1640–1830*. Setauket, N.Y.: Society for the Preservation of Long Island Antiquities, 1976.

Finkelstein, Barbara, and Kathy Vandell. "The Schooling of American Childhood: The Emergence of Learning Communities, 1820–1920." In *A Century of Childhood: 1820–1920*. Rochester, N.Y.: The Margaret Woodbury Strong Museum, 1984.

Flick, Alexander C., ed. *History of the State of New York in Ten Volumes*. New York: Columbia University Press, 1935.

Fox, Sandi. *Wrapped in Glory: Figurative Quilts & Bedcovers 1700-1900*. New York: Thames and Hudson, 1990.

Gass, Margaret Davis. *History of Miller's Place*. Long Island: privately printed, 1971 (revised 1987).

Gerard, Helene. *Needles and Thread: Jewish Life in Suffolk County*. Stony Brook, N.Y.: Long Island Studies Council, 1986.

Goerlich, Shirley Boyce. *Genealogy: A Practical Research Guide*. Sidney, N.Y.: RSG Publishing, 1984.

Gottesman, Rita Susswein. *The Arts and Crafts in New York, 1726-1776: Advertisements and News Items from New York City Newspapers*. New York: The New-York Historical Society, 1938.

_____, *The Arts and Crafts in New York, 1800-1804: Advertisements and News Items from New York City Newspapers*. New York: The New-York Historical Society, 1965.

Green, Harvey. *The Light of the Home: An Intimate View of the Lives of Women in Victorian America*. New York: Pantheon Books, 1983.

Gunn, Virginia. "Dress Fabrics of the Late Nineteenth Century." In *Bits and Pieces: Textile Traditions*. Edited by Jeannette Lasansky. Lewisburg, Pa.: Oral Traditions Project of the Union County Historical Society, 1991.

Haders, Phyllis. *The Warner's Collector's Guide to American Quilts*. Pittstown, N.J.: Main Street Press, 1981.

Hall, Carrie A., and Rose G. Kretsinger. *The Romance of the Patchwork Quilt in America in Three Parts*. New York: Bonanza Books, 1935.

Harrison, Gabriel. *John Howard Payne, Dramatist, Poet, Actor and Author of Home Sweet Home: His Life and Writings*. Philadelphia: J.P. Lippincott, 1855.

Hartley, Miss Florence. *Ladies Hand Book of Fancy and Ornamental Work*. Philadelphia, 1859.

Hayden, Dolores. *The Great Domestic Revolution: A History of Feminist Designs for American Homes, Neighborhoods, and Cities*. Cambridge: The MIT Press, 1981.

Hinds, William Alfred. *American Communities and Cooperative Colonies*. 2d rev. ed. Philadelphia: Porcupine Press, 1975.

Hinson, Dolores. *Quilting Manual*. New York: Dover Publications, 1966.

Holstein, Jonathan. *The Pieced Quilt: An American Design Tradition*. Boston: Little, Brown & Co., 1982.

Horne, Field, ed. *The Diary of Molly Cooper: Life on a Long Island Farm 1768-1773*. Oyster Bay, N.Y.: Oyster Bay Historical Society, 1981.

Howe, John B. *The New York State Fair, Its Genesis and Its History*. Syracuse: Hall & McChesney, 1917.

Hudson, Winthrop S. *Religion in America*, 2d ed. New York: Charles Scribner's Sons, 1973.

Hurd, Charles. *The Compact History of the American Red Cross*. New York: Hawthorn Books, 1959.

Jones, Louis C. *Three Eyes on the Past: Exploring New York Folk Life*. Syracuse: Syracuse University Press, 1982.

Khin, Yvonne M. *The Collector's Dictionary of Quilt Names & Patterns* (Washington, D.C.: Acropolis Books Ltd., 1980)

King's Handbook of New York City 1893. 2d enlarged ed. Vol. 1. New York: Benjamin Blom, reissued 1972.

Kolter, Jane Bentley. *Forget Me Not: A Gallery of Friendship and Album Quilts*. Pittstown, N.J.: The Main Street Press, 1985.

Lasansky, Jeannette. *In the Heart of Pennsylvania: 19th and 20th Century Quiltmaking Traditions*. Lewisburg, Pa.: Oral Traditions Project of the Union County Historical Society, 1985.

_____. *Pieced by Mother: Over 100 Years of Quiltmaking Traditions*. Lewisburg, Pa.: Oral Traditions Project of the Union County Historical Society, 1987.

_____ et al. *Bits and Pieces: Textile Traditions*. Lewisburg, Pa.: An Oral Traditions Project of the Union County Historical Society, 1991.

Laury, Jean Ray. *Ho for California! Pioneer Women and Their Quilts*. New York: E. P. Dutton, 1990.

Lichten, Frances. *Decorative Art of Victoria's Era*. New York: Charles Scribner's Sons, 1950.

Lowitt, Richard, and Maurine Beasley, eds. *One Third of a Nation: Lorena Hickok Reports on the Great Depression*. Urbana, Ill.: University of Illinois Press, 1981.

Ludwig, Allan I. *Graven Images: New England Stonecarving and Its Symbols: 1650-1815*. Middletown, Conn.: Wesleyan University Press, 1966.

Lynes, Russell. *The Tastemakers: The Shaping of American Popular Taste*. New York: Dover Publications, 1980.

MacDowell, Marsha, and C. Kurt Dewhurst. "Expanding Frontiers: The Michigan Folk Art Project." In *Perspectives on American Folk Art*. Edited by Ian M.G. Quimby and Scott T. Swank. New York: W.W. Norton & Co., 1980.

_____, and Ruth D. Fitzgerald. *Michigan Quilts: 150 Years of a Textile Tradition*. East Lansing: Michigan State University Museum, 1987.

Massey, Mary Elizabeth. *Bonnet Brigades*. New York: Alfred A. Knopf, 1966.

Malone, Maggie. *1001 Patchwork Designs* New York: Sterling Publishing Co., Inc., 1982.

Mau, Clinton. *The Development of Central and Western New York From the Arrival of the White Man to the Eve of the Civil War*. Dansville, N.Y.: F.A. Owen Publishing Co., 1958.

McMorris, Penny. *Crazy Quilts*. New York: E. P. Dutton, 1984.

McPherson, James M. *Battle Cry of Freedom: The Civil War Era*. New York: Oxford University Press, 1988.

Merrill, Arch. *The Towpath*. Rochester, N.Y.: The Gannett Co., 1945.

Miller, Mary Esther Mulford. *An East Hampton Childhood*. East Hampton, N.Y.: Star Press, n.d.

Montgomery, Florence M. *Textiles in America 1650-1870*. New York: W.W. Norton & Co., 1984.

Mrs. Child. *The Little Girl's Own Book*. n.p., 1840.

Mrs. Pullan. *The Lady's Manual of Fancy Work*. New York: n.p., 1858.

Newman, Thelma R. *Quilting, Patchwork, Appliqué, and Trapunto: Traditional Methods and Original Designs*. New York: Crown Publishers, 1974.

Nordhoff, Charles. *The Communistic Societies of the United States: From Personal Visit and Observation*. New York: Harper & Brothers, 1875.

Noyes, Marion F., ed. *A History of Schoharie County*. Schoharie, N.Y.: Schoharie County Historical Society, 1980.

Noyes, Russell. *English Romantic Poetry and Prose*. New York:

Oxford University Press, 1956.

Orlofsky, Patsy and Myron. *Quilts in America*. New York: McGraw-Hill, 1974.

Oshins, Lisa Turner. *Quilt Collections: A Directory for the United States and Canada*. Washington, D.C.: Acropolis Books, Ltd., 1987.

Peck, Amelia. *American Quilts & Coverlets in The Metropolitan Museum of Art*. New York: Dutton Studio Books, 1990.

Pettit, Florence H. *America's Printed & Painted Fabrics: 1600–1900*. New York: Hastings House, 1970.

Rae, Janet. *Quilts of the British Isles*. New York: E. P. Dutton, 1987.

Ramsey, Bets, and Merikay Waldvogel. *The Quilts of Tennessee: Images of Domestic Life Prior to 1930*. Nashville, Tenn.: Rutledge Hill Press, 1986.

Rattray, Jeannette Edwards. *East Hampton History Including Genealogies of Early Families*. East Hampton, N.Y.: privately published, 1953.

————. *Ship Ashore! A Record of Maritime Disasters*. New York: Coward McCann, 1955.

Rawson, Elizabeth Reich. "An Analysis of Selected Inventories for Household Furnishings and Room Use From Suffolk County, NY 1658 to 1741." In *Long Island Studies: Evoking a Sense of Place*. Edited by Joann P. Krieg. Interlaken, N.Y. Heart of the Lakes Publishing, 1988.

Rehmel, Judy. *Key to 1000 Quilt Patterns*, 1978.

Reed, William Howell. *The Heroic Story of the U.S. Sanitary Commission, 1861–1865*. Boston: G. H. Ellis, n.d.

Richards, Caroline Cowles. *Village Life in America, 1852–1872*. New York: Henry Holt and Company, 1908.

Roberson, Ruth Haislip, ed. *North Carolina Quilts*. Chapel Hill: University of North Carolina Press, 1988.

Rossano, Geoffrey L. "To Market, To Market. Oyster Bay and the International Economy in the mid-Eighteenth Century." In *Long Island Studies: Evoking a Sense of Place*. Edited by Joann P. Krieg. Interlaken, N.Y.: Heart of the Lakes Publishing, 1988.

Safford, Carleton L. and Robert Bishop. *America's Quilts and Coverlets*. New York: E. P. Dutton, 1972.

Samuels, Peggy and Harold. *Frederic Remington: A Biography*. Garden City, N.Y.: Doubleday & Co., 1982.

Schoeser, Mary, and Celia Rufey. *English and American Textiles from 1790 to the Present*. New York: Thames & Hudson, 1989.

Schramm, Henry W. *Empire Showcase: A History of the New York State Fair*. Utica, N.Y.: North Country Books, 1985.

Smith, George Winston, and Charles Judah. *Life In the North During the Civil War: A Source History*. Albuquerque: University of New Mexico Press, 1966.

Strasser, Susan. *Never Done: A History of American Housework*. New York: Pantheon Books, 1982.

Swan, Susan Burrows. *Plain and Fancy: American Women and Their Needlework, 1700–1850*. New York: Holt, Rinehart & Winston, 1977.

The Young Lady's Friend, n.p., 1837.

Thompson, Benjamin F. *History of Long Island From Its Discovery and Settlement to the Present*. 3d ed. Vol. 2. New York: Robert H. Dodd, 1918.

Thompson, John H., ed. *Geography of New York State*. Syracuse: Syracuse University Press, 1966.

Valentine, Helen G. and Andrus T. *An Island's People: One Foot in the Sea, One on Shore*. Huntington, N.Y.: Peterson Press and Associates, 1976.

Van Wagenen, Jr., Jared. *The Golden Age of Homespun*. Ithaca: Cornell University Press, 1960.

Walton, Frank L. *Tomahawks to Textiles: The Fabulous Story of Worth Street*. New York: Appleton-Century-Crofts, 1953.

Warner, George H. *Military Records of Schoharie Veterans of Four Wars*. Albany: privately published, 1891.

Weissman, Judith Reiter, and Wendy Lavitt. *Labors of Love: America's Textiles and Needlework, 1650–1930*. New York: Alfred A. Knopf, 1987.

Werdman, Bette S., and Linda B. Martin. *Nassau County, Long Island, in Early Photographs: 1869–1940*. New York: Dover Publications, 1981.

Westin, Jeanne. *Making Do: How Women Survived the '30s*. Chicago: Follett Publishing Company, 1976.

Whiting, Gertrude. *Tools and Toys of Stitchery*. New York: Columbia University Press, 1928.

Willard, Frances E., and Mary A. Livermore, eds. *A Woman of the Century. Fourteen Hundred-Seventy Biographical Sketches Accompanied by Portraits of Leading American Women In All Walks of Life*. Buffalo, N.Y.: Charles Wells Moulton, 1893. Republished by Gale Research Company, Detroit, 1967.

Williams, Sherman. *New York's Part in History*. New York: D. Appleton & Co., 1915.

Wilson, Kax. *A History of Textiles*. Boulder, Colo.: Westview Press, 1979.

Woodard, Thos K. and Blanche Greenstein. *Twentieth Century Quilts: 1900–1950*. New York: E. P. Dutton, 1988.

Wright, Julia McNair, *The Complete Home: An Encyclopedia of Domestic Life and Affairs*. Philadelphia: J.C. McCurdy & Co., 1879.

Wyld, Lionel D. *Low Bridge: Folklore and the Erie Canal*. Syracuse, N.Y.: Syracuse University Press, 1962.

Yeager, Edna Howell. *Peconic River Mills and Industries*. Riverhead, N.Y.: Suffolk County Historical Society, 1965.

Periodicals, Magazines, Newspapers:

Curtis, Philip H. "American Quilts in the Newark Museum Collection." *The Museum New Series* 25, nos. 3-4, Summer-Fall, 1973.

Davis, General George W. "The Sanitary Commission—Red Cross." *Journal of International Law*, July 1910.

Federico, Jean Taylor. "White Work Classification System." *Uncoverings 1980*. Mill Valley, Calif.: American Quilt Study Group, 1981, 68-71.

Fowler, William B., ed. *The Common School Journal New Series* 12, no. 1, 10, no. 18, and 9. Boston: Fitz, Hobbs & Co., 1850. Microfilm, New York Public Library.

Foudji, Gazo. "A Dragon Quilt." *Ladies' Home Journal*, May 1905. Microfilm Reels 757-766, New York Public Library.

Fox, Sandi. "The Log Cabin: An American Quilt on the Western Frontier." *The Quilt Digest*. San Francisco: 1983, 6-13.

Fratto, Toni Flores. "Remember Me: The Sources of American Sampler Verses." *New York Folklore* 2, Winter 1976, 205-222.

Godey's Lady's Book. "Patchwork." March 1851.

Gunn, Virginia. "Quilts for Union Soldiers in the Civil War." *Uncoverings 1985*. Mill Valley, Calif.: American Quilt Study Group, 1986, 95-121.

_____. "Yo-Yo or Bed of Roses Quilts: Nineteenth Century Origins." *Uncoverings 1987*. Mill Valley, Calif.: American Quilt Study Group, 1988, 129-146.

Harper's Bazar. 2 November; 7, 14 December 1867; 14, 21 March; 18 April 1868; 21 December 1872; 13 September 1884. Microfilm Reels 430-450, New York Public Library.

Heritage 7, no. 6, July/August, 1991. "General Store Operations." Cooperstown: New York State Historical Association.

Heritage 7, no. 6, July/August, 1991. "Twin Counties Mark Two Hundred Years." Cooperstown: New York State Historical Association.

Ladies' Home Journal. "You Might Consider Making a 'Bible Quilt.'" August 1938.

Lanigan, Sybil. "Revival of the Patchwork Quilt." *Ladies' Home Journal*, October 1894. Microfilm Reels 755-766, New York Public Library.

Mathieson, Judy. "Some Published Sources of Design Inspiration for the Quilt Pattern Mariner's Compass—17th to 20th Century." *Uncoverings 1981*. Mill Valley, Calif.: American Quilt Study Group, 1982, 11-18.

Meyer, Suellen. "Early Influences of the Sewing Machine and Visible Machine Stitching on Nineteenth-Century Quilts." *Uncoverings 1989*. San Francisco: American Quilt Study Group, 1990, 38-52.

_____. "Pine Tree Quilts." *Quilt Digest 4*. San Francisco: Quilt Digest Press, 1986, 6-19.

Miss Leslie. "Orphelina: A Tale." *Miss Leslie's Magazine* 1, n.p. March 1843.

Moore's Rural-New Yorker, Rochester: 23 September 1854; 16 August 1855; 2 January 1858; 7 January 1860; 5 September 1863; 4 March 1865.

Nickols, Pat L. "The Use of Cotton Sacks in Quiltmaking." *Uncoverings 1988*. San Francisco: American Quilt Study Group, 1989, 57-71.

Parsons, Karen, ed. "The History of the Old Trade School." *Quarterly* 20, no. 1. Huntington, N.Y.: Huntington Historical Society, Fall 1980.

Peterson's, June, July, August, October, and November 1861.

Peto, Florence. "Three Generations of Quilts." *The Magazine Antiques*. June 1944, 306-307.

Prescott, Augusta Salisbury. "Our Spare Room." *Godey's Lady's Book*, April 1889.

Robinson, Edith. "The Best Housekeeper in Banbury." *Ladies' Home Journal*. June 1905. Microfilm Reels 755-766, New York Public Library.

Seal, Ethel Davis. "Old Patchwork Revival." *Ladies' Home Journal*, August 1920.

Sickels, Elizabeth Galbraith. "New York Thimble Makers From Huntington, Long Island." *The Antiques Journal*. September 1964, 13-17; October 1964, 18-23; and November 1964, 21-26.

The Cultivator, Albany 4, 1837; 8, 1841; 10, no. 10, 1843; 11, no. 10, 1844; 12, no. 10, 1845; 13, no. 9, 1846.

The Household Journal. October 13, 1860.

The Lady's Book 1, Philadelphia: L.A. Godey & Co., 1830.

The Real Estate Record and Builders Guide. 35-101. New York: New-York Historical Society Collections, 1885.

Trechsel, Gail Andrews. "Mourning Quilts in America." *Uncoverings 1989*. San Francisco: American Quilt Study Group, 1990, 139-158.

Weston, Richard. "'Apple Bee' and 'Quilting Bee' in New York State in the 1830s." *The American Magazine, and Historical Chronicle* 1, Spring-Summer 1988. Ann Arbor: William L. Clements Library, The University of Michigan.

Zegart, Shelly. "Old Maid, New Woman." *The Quilt Digest*. San Francisco: The Quilt Digest Press, 1986, 54-65.

Exhibition Catalogues:

Buff, Barbara Ball, ed. *A Celebration of Westchester: Art and Decoration of Three Hundred Years*. Scarsdale, N.Y.: The Scarsdale Historical Society, 1981.

Chittenden, Varick A. *Stitches in Time: Heirloom Quilts and Coverlets of Northern New York*. Malone, N.Y.: Ballard Mill Center for the Arts, 1983.

de Julio, Mary Antoine. "What a Rich Reward!" In *Betsey Reynolds Voorhees and the Collection of Her Handiwork*. Fort Johnson, N.Y.: Montgomery County Historical Society, 1986.

Horton, Laurel, and Lynn Robertson Myers. *South Carolina's Traditional Quilts*. Columbia: McKissick Museum, University of South Carolina, 1984.

Ice, Joyce, and Linda Norris, eds. *Quilted Together: Women, Quilts, and Communities*. Delhi, N.Y.: The Delaware County Historical Association, 1989.

Macneal, Patricia Miner, and Maude Southwell Wahlman. *Quilts From Appalachia*. Pennsylvania: Palmer Museum of Art, Pennsylvania State University, 1988.

Masonic Symbols in American Decorative Arts. Lexington, Mass.: Scottish Rite Masonic Museum of Our National Heritage, 1976.

Pike, Martha V. and Janice Gray Armstrong. *Time to Mourn: Expressions of Grief in Nineteenth Century America*. Stony Brook, N.Y.: The Museums at Stony Brook, 1980.

Rettew, Gayle A., William H. Siener, and Janice Tauer Weiss. "Behold the Labour of my Tender Age, Children and Their Samplers, 1780–1850." Rochester, N.Y.: Rochester Museum and Science Center, 1983.

Schwoeffermann, Catherine. *Sound Avenue Ladies*. Riverhead, N.Y.: Hallockville Folk Museum, 1988.

Encyclopedias, Directories, and Dictionaries:

Caulfeild, S.F.A., and Blanche C. Saward. *The Dictionary of Needlework: An Encyclopedia of Artistic, Plain, and Fancy Needlework*. London: L. Upcott Gill, 1882.

Columbia Encyclopedia, 2d ed., s.v. "Spanish-American War."

Dictionary of American Biography, 1936 ed., s.v. "Frances Elizabeth Caroline Willard."

Dictionary of American Biography, 1936 ed., s.v. "Elkanah Watson."

The Blue Book Textile Directory of the United States and Canada. New York: Davison Publishing Co., 1899–1940.

Wingate, Isabel B., ed. *Fairchild's Dictionary of Textiles*. New York: Fairchild Publications, 1974.

Diaries, Letters, and Family Papers:

Adams, Abigail. Letter to John Adams, March 31, 1776.

Massachusetts Historical Society, Boston.

Dominy, Phoebe. Letter to Temperance Dominy, November 19, 1837. East Hampton Free Library, The Long Island Collection, East Hampton, N.Y.

Dunstan, Caroline A. Diaries, 1856–1870. Manuscript Division of the Research Libraries of the New York Public Library, New York City.

Helme, Eliza. Letter to Mother, October 4, 1806. East Hampton Free Library, The Long Island Collection, East Hampton, N.Y.

Terry, Henrietta. Diary Entries for years 1883 and 1884. Collection of Suffolk County Historical Society, Riverhead, N.Y.

Thompson, Dr. Samuel L. Diary, 1800–1808. Collection of Society for Preservation of Long Island Antiquities, Setauket, N.Y.

Watkins Family Papers. Manuscript Division of the Research Libraries of the New York Public Library.

White, Tryphena Ely. Journal. Privately published, 1904. New-York Historical Society.

Reports and Interviews:

Aldrich, Hattie Downs. Interview by Phyllis A. Tepper and Aurelie Stack. Riverhead, 7 July 1988. Tape recording, Museum of American Folk Art, New York.

Collins, Ellen. *Women's Central Association of Relief Table of Supplies Received and Distributed from May 1st 1861 to July 7th, 1865* in WRHS Manuscript 1012. Container 10, Folder 6.

Vreeland, Joella. "The Southold Sisterhood—Sociables and Serious Business." Southold, N.Y.: Academy Printing Services, 1985.

Unpublished Papers:

Bloom, Joan. "Delectable Mountain Quilt of Aurelia Loomis Root." Folk Art Institute, Museum of American Folk Art, 1991.

Fisher, Nancy. "Sampler Quilt made by Mary Catherine Dearborn Close." Folk Art Institute, Museum of American Folk Art, 1990.

Hill, Diane. "Feathered Star Variation Quilt of Ellen McKnight Brayton." Folk Art Institute, Museum of American Folk Art, 1991.

Hohenrath, Caroline. "Crazy Quilt of Josephine Cashman Hooker." Folk Art Institute, Museum of American Folk Art, 1991.

Kuhlthau, Carolyn. "The Hoppey-Whiting Crazy Quilt in the Fan Pattern." Folk Art Institute, Museum of American Folk Art, 1989.

Lieu, Fran. "Candace Wheeler." Folk Art Institute, Museum of American Folk Art, 1991.

Noyes, Marion F. "Early Academies and Seminaries of Schoharie County." Master's thesis, 1938.

Snook, Sarah. "The Miller Place, Long Island Sampler Quilt." Folk Art Institute, Museum of American Folk Art, 1990.

Steuer, Lynne. "Princess Feather with Cherry Trees." Folk Art Institute, Museum of American Folk Art, 1991.

Indices

GENERAL INDEX

(**Bold Face** indicates an illustrated reference)

INDEX OF MAKERS OF NEW YORK STATE QUILTS

(**Bold face** indicates photograph of quiltmaker)

INDEX OF QUILT PHOTOGRAPHS

(The following list includes the names of all quilts illustrated in the book.
All other references to patterns and designs appear in the general index.)